Welcome to the World Heritage C

Ite.
sho
bo
tele
barc
This
Re
Fi
i
be
L

...e are places that somehow manage ...nder your skin, even though you ...ally know them all that well. ... is that kind of place. A warm and ... place, a place made for people. ...ose history made it great, re- ...a well-de... classification ...sco World Heritage site.

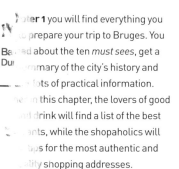

...is guide you will discover Bruges ...nt facets. There are five separate ...rs.

...ter 1 you will find everything you ...o prepare your trip to Bruges. You ...d about the ten *must sees*, get a ...mary of the city's history and ...ots of practical information. ...n this chapter, the lovers of good ...drink will find a list of the best ...nts, while the shopaholics will ...ps for the most authentic and ...ity shopping addresses.

...e inspiring walking routes in- ...**chapter 2** will take you to all ...beautiful spots in town. The ...ed **city plan** – which you can sim- ...d out of the back cover of this ...will make sure that you don't ...r way.

...apter **3** provides a summary of the ...ny different possibilities for explor- ...Bruges and gives details of every- ...g the city has to offer in cultural ...ms: a calendar of the most impor-

the Bruges museums, attractions and other sites of interest, including histor-ical, cultural and religious buildings and locations. Bruges' beautiful squares and enchanting canals are the regular backdrop for topclass cultural events. And few cities have such a rich and diverse variety of museums, which contain gems ranging from the Flemish primitives and beautiful lacework to the finest modern art of today.

In Bruges you can dine at a different star-rated restaurant each day, or per-haps you would prefer lunch at a trendy bistro before wandering through the winding cobbled streets of the city? Or maybe you just want to take in a pleasant pub or one of the many magnificent ter-races with a view? These are the places, full of charm and character, which you can read about in **chapter 4**. Five 'new arrivals' to the city will also tell you about their favourite places in town.

Staying a bit longer in the region? **Chapter 5** suggests a number of excur-sions to the other Flemish historical cities, the Bruges Wetlands and Wood-lands, the coast, the Westhoek, the Lys valley, the Meetjesland (Creek Country) and the Flemish Ardennes.
    The choice is yours!

Belfry

Discover
Bruges

Highlights of Bruges
The 10 'classics' you don't want to miss

〰 Rozenhoedkaai and the Bruges canals, a typical city view

The Rozenhoedkaai (Rosary Quay) links the Belfry with the city's network of canals, the true 'veins' of Bruges, and offers a unique and picturesque panoramic view. Hardly surprising, then, that the Rozenhoedkaai is the most popular photographic hot-spot in town! You can discover many more special places and hidden pearls during a boat trip on the canals. From the water, Bruges is even more enchanting. A classic that you really don't want to miss.

🐎 Markt: an absolute must

The vibrant centre of the city has been dominated for centuries by the 83-metre high Belfry. Today, you can climb right to the top of this impressive tower. You will be rewarded with a spectacular view of Bruges and the surrounding countryside. The Markt (Market Square) is also home to the Historium, a top attraction that takes you back in time to the city's medi-

eval past. Ringed with colourful houses, the Market Square is also the regular standing place for the famous horse-drawn carriages.

(Read more on pages 76 and 84-85)

Medieval splendour on the Burg

The Burg is the beating heart of the city. From the 14th century town hall, which is the oldest in the Low Countries, Bruges has been governed for more than 600 years. This majestic architectural square also contains the Palace of the Liberty of Bruges, the former Civil Registry and the Basilica of the Holy Blood.

No other location in Bruges bears greater testimony to the city's former wealth. *(Read more on pages 75, 79 and 92)*

Strolling through the old Hansa Quarter

From the 13th to the 15th century, Bruges was the most important trading centre in North-West Europe. Spanish merchants settled along the Spaanse Loskaai (Spanish Quay) and in the Spanjaardstraat. The Germans or Easterners – 'oosterlingen' in Dutch – took up residence in the Oosterlingenplein. In this old Hansa Quarter you can admire the mansions of the wealthy international merchants and the great trading nations of the day. You can almost still smell the atmosphere of the Middle Ages.

The Flemish primitives: timeless beauty

In Bruges' Golden Age – the 15th century – art was king. Leading artists of the day, like Jan van Eyck and Hans Memling, came to live and work in the city. Today, you can marvel at the masterpieces of the world-famous Flemish primitives in the Groeninge Museum and the St. John's Hospital. Here you can come face to face with the great paintings that were created in the city all those centuries ago.
(Read more on pages 84 and 90)

7

Church of Our Lady: a work of beauty in brick

The Onze-Lieve-Vrouwekerk (Church of Our Lady), with its imposing 115.5-metre high brick tower, is not only a fine testimony to the skill of the Bruges master builders of yesteryear, but is also the second tallest brick church spire in the world. Inside the church visitors will be moved by the magnificence of Michelangelo's white marble *Madonna and Child*.
(Read more on pages 86-87)

Quiet contemplation in the Beguinage

Some places are so beautiful that they leave you speechless. The Beguinage is just such a place. This is where the beguines – emancipated women who lived pious and chaste lives without taking holy orders – once lived together in harmony. This walled oasis of religious peace, with it delightful inner garden, wind-twisted trees and white-painted gables, can charm even the most cynical of souls with its deafening silence. *(Read more on page 75-76)*

8

Minnewater:
romance all the way

This small rectangular lake was once the mooring place for the barges that sailed the inland waterways between Bruges and Ghent. Nowadays, together with the Minnewater Park, this stretch of water – whose name means Lake of love – is the most romantic spot in the city. The Minnewater Bridge offers magical views over one of the most idyllic places in Bruges.

Concert Hall or Culture with a capital C

This tall and stately culture temple on 't Zand gives the square its own unique dynamism. In the soberly decorated auditorium, visitors can enjoy classical music and contemporary dance in the best possible setting. This international music and arts centre is already famed for the excellence of its acoustics. *(Read more on pages 80 and 95)*

🏠 Almshouses:
charity embodied in stone

Villages within the city. That is how you could best describe these medieval residential centres, which are still inhabited today. Centuries ago, the almshouses were built from charitable funds for the care of the impoverished elderly or retired craftsmen. Today, with their picturesque gardens, their white-painted gables and their delicious peace and quiet, they are amongst the most restful places in Bruges. *(Read more on page 38)*

History in a nutshell

The Market Square in Bruges, 17th century
(painting by Jan-Baptist Meunincxhove)

Water played a crucial role in the birth and development of Bruges. At the place where the city was first born, a number of streams flowed together to form a river (the River Reie), which then ran northwards through the coastal plain. Through a series of tidal creeks, the river eventually reached the sea. Little wonder, then, that even as far back as Roman times there was already considerable seafaring activity in this region. This has been proven by the discovery of the remains of two seagoing ships from this period, dating from the second half of the 3rd century or the first half of the 4th century. Even so, it would be another five centuries before the name 'Bruges' first began to appear – the word being a deriva-

Its growing importance also resulted in it becoming the main fortified residence of the counts of Flanders, so that from the 11th century onwards the city was not only a prosperous trading metropolis, but also a seat of considerable political power.

Taking off

When the city's direct link with the sea was in danger of silting-up in the 12th century, Bruges went through a period of anxiety. Fortunately, the new waterway of the Zwin brought relief. As a result, Bruges was able to call itself the most important trade centre of North-west Europe in the following century. The world's first ever stock exchange ('Beurs' in Dutch) was also founded in Bruges. These market activities took place in the square in front of the house owned by a powerful local family of brokers, the Van der Beurse family. As a result, their name became linked for all time with this kind of financial institution. In spite of the typical medieval maladies, from epidemics to political unrest and social inequality, the citizens of Bruges prospered, and soon the city developed a magnet-like radiation. Around 1340, the inner city numbered no fewer than 35.000 inhabitants.

Golden Age

Success continually increased. In the 15th century – Bruges' Golden Age – things improved further when the Royal House of Burgundy took up residence in the city. New luxury goods were produced and sold in abundance, and famous painters such as Jan van Eyck and Hans Memling – the great Flemish primitives – found their creative niche here.

The fine arts flourished, and besides a substantial number of fine churches and unique merchant houses, a monumental town hall was also erected. Bruges' success seemed imperishable.

Decline

The sudden death in 1482 of the much-loved ruler, Mary of Burgundy, heralded the start of new and less fortunate times for the city. The relationship between the citizens of Bruges and their lord, the widower Maximilian, turned sour. The Burgundian court left the city, with the international traders following in its wake. Long centuries of wars and changes of political power took their toll. By the middle of the 19th century Bruges had become an impoverished city. Strangely enough, its fortunes were changed for the better by the writing of a novel.

Revival

With great care, Bruges took its first steps into tourism. In *Bruges la Morte* (1892), Georges Rodenbach aptly describes Bruges as a somewhat sleepy, yet extremely mysterious place. Above all, the 35 photographs included in the book made its readers curious about what they might find. Soon Bruges' magnificent patrimony was rediscovered and its mysterious intimacy turned out to be its greatest asset. Building on this enthusiasm, the city was provided with a new seaport, which was called Zeebrugge. The pulling power of Bruges proved to be a great success and UNESCO added the medieval city centre to its World Heritage list. The rest is history.

From early settlement to international trade centre
(...-1200)

851 Earliest record of the city
863 Baldwin I takes up residence at Burg square
1127 Charles the Good, Count of Flanders, is murdered in the Church of Saint Donatian; first town rampart; first Bruges city charter
1134 Creation of the Zwin – evolving from the Sincfal marshes – that links Damme with the sea

Bruges' Golden Age
(1369-1500)

1369 Margaret of Dampierre marries Philip the Bold, Duke of Burgundy. Beginning of the Burgundian period
1384 Margaret succeeds her father Louis of Male
1430 Marriage of Duke Philip the Good with Isabella of Portugal; establishment of the Order of the Golden Fleece
1436 Jan van Eyck paints the panel *Madonna with Canon Joris van der Paele*
1482 Mary of Burgundy dies as a result of a fall with her horse
1488 Maximilian of Austria is locked up in Craenenburg House on Markt for a few weeks

851 1200 1300 1500

Bruges as the economic capital of Northwest Europe
(1200-1400)

1245 Foundation of the Beguinage
1280 Reconstruction in stone of the Belfry after the destruction of its wooden predecessor
1297 Second town rampart
1302 Bruges Matins and Battle of the Golden Spurs
1304 First Procession of the Holy Blood
1376-1420 Construction of the City Hall

The city gets her second wind
(1500-1578)

1506 The cloth merchants Jan and Alexander Mouscron buy Michelangelo's *Madonna and Child*
1528 Lancelot Blondeel designs the mantelpiece of the Liberty of Bruges
1548 Birth of the scientist Simon Stevin
1562 Marcus Gerards engraves the first printed town map of Bruges
1578 Bruges joins the rebellion against the Spanish king

An impoverished town in a pauperised Flanders (1584-1885)

1584 Bruges becomes reconciled with the Spanish king
1604 The Zwin is closed off
1713-1795 Austrian period
1717 Foundation of the Academy of Fine Arts, which formed the basis for the collection of the Groeninge Museum.
1795-1814 French period
1799 Demolition of Saint Donatian's Cathedral and renovation of Burg
1815-1830 United Kingdom of the Netherlands
1830 Independence of Belgium; birth of Guido Gezelle
1838 First railway line in Bruges inaugurated on 't Zand

The new city (1971-...)

1971 Amalgamation Law incorporates former suburbs
1985 King Baudouin opens new sea lock at Zeebrugge
2000 Historic city centre is given World Heritage status; Euro 2000 (European Football Championship)
2002 European Capital of Culture
2008 *In Bruges* is released worldwide in cinemas
2009 The Procession of the Holy Blood is granted Intangible Cultural Heritage status by UNESCO
2013 Bruges is the setting for the Bollywood blockbuster *Peekay*
2016 Bruges' De Halve Maan Brewery opens the first underground beer pipeline in the world.

1600   1700   1800   1900   2000

Provincial town with revived ambitions (1885-1970)

1887 Unveiling of the statue of Jan Breydel and Pieter de Coninck (Markt)
1892 Publication of *Bruges la Morte* by Georges Rodenbach
1896 Start of the construction of the seaport
1897 Dutch becomes the official language

1902 First important exhibition of the Flemish primitives
1914-1918 The Great War: Bruges is a German naval base
1940-1945 The historic city centre survives Second World War almost unscathed
1958 First Pageant of the Golden Tree

Practical information

Accessibility

If you see the symbol ♿ in this guide, this means that provision has been made for people with disabilities. Further details about the level of accessibility can be found at the ℹ tourist information offices.

Bicycle rental points

» 🚲 📶 **Bauhaus Bike Rental**
LOCATION > Langestraat 145
PRICE > 3 hours: € 6.00; full day: € 10.00
OPEN > Daily, 8.00 a.m.-9.00 p.m. (bikes must be returned by 9.00 p.m.)
INFO > Tel. +32 (0)50 34 10 93,
www.bauhaus.be/services/bike-rental

» 🚲 **B-Bike Concertgebouw**
LOCATION > Concertgebouw, 't Zand
PRICE > 1 hour: € 4.00; 5 hours: € 8.00;
full day: € 12.00. Tandem, 5 hours: € 14.00;

full day: € 22.00. Electric bike, full day:
€ 20.00
OPEN > During the period 1/3 to 1/12: daily,
10.00 a.m.-7.00 p.m.
INFO > Tel. +32 (0)479 97 12 80,
info@b-bike.be

» 🚲 **Bruges Bike Rental**
LOCATION > Niklaas Desparsstraat 17
PRICE > 1 hour: € 4.00; 2 hours: € 7.00;
4 hours: € 10.00; full day: € 13.00, students
(on display of a valid student card): € 10.00.
Tandem, 1 hour: € 10.00; 2 hours: € 15.00;
4 hours: € 20.00; full day: € 25.00, students
(on display of a valid student card): € 22.00
OPEN > During the period 1/2 to 31/12: daily,
10.00 a.m.-8.00 p.m.
ADDITIONAL CLOSING DATES >
1/1 and 25/12
INFO > Tel. +32 (0)50 61 61 08,
www.brugesbikerental.be

» De Ketting
LOCATION > Gentpoortstraat 23
PRICE > Full day: € 7.00. Electric bike, full day: € 20.00
OPEN > During the period 1/4 to 15/10: Monday to Saturday, 10.00 a.m.-6.00 p.m. and Sunday, 10.30 a.m.-6.00 p.m.; during the period 16/10 to 31/3: Monday to Saturday, 10.00 a.m.-6.00 p.m.
INFO > Tel. +32 (0)50 34 41 96, www.deketting.be

» Electric Scooters
Rental of electric bikes.
LOCATION > Gentpoortstraat 55 en 62
PRICE > 2 hours: € 10.00; 4 hours: € 18.00; full day: € 30.00
OPEN > During the period 1/4 to 31/10: Wednesday to Saturday, 10.00 a.m.-6.00 p.m.
EXTRA > Rental of electric scooters *(see pages 20-21)*
INFO > Tel. +32 (0)474 09 19 18, www.electric-scooters.be

» Eric Popelier
LOCATION > Mariastraat 26
PRICE > 1 hour: € 5.00; 4 hours: € 10.00; full day: € 15.00. Electric bike or tandem, 1 hour: € 10.00; 4 hours: € 20.00; full day: € 30.00
OPEN > During the period 15/3 to 15/10: daily, 9.00 a.m.-7.00 p.m.; during the period 16/10 to 14/3: daily, 10.00 a.m.-6.00 p.m.
ADDITIONAL CLOSING DATES >
1/1, 25/5 and 25/12, closed on Monday in January and December
INFO > Tel. +32 (0)50 34 32 62, www.fietsenpopelier.be

» Fietspunt Station
LOCATION > Hendrik Brugmansstraat 3 (Stationsplein)
PRICE > 1 hour: € 6.00; 4 hours: € 10.00; full day: € 15.00. Electric bike, 4 hours: € 20.00; full day: € 30.00
OPEN > Monday to Friday, 7.00 a.m-7.00 p.m.; during the period 1/5 to 30/9:

also during weekends and on holidays, 9.00 a.m.-8.00 p.m.
ADDITIONAL CLOSING DATES >
1/1 to 3/1 and 25/12 to 31/12
INFO > Tel. +32 (0)50 39 68 26 fietspunt.brugge@groepintro.be

» Koffieboontje
LOCATION > Hallestraat 4
PRICE > 1 hour: € 5.00; 4 hours: € 10.00; full day: € 15.00, students (on display of a valid student card): € 11.25. Tandem, 1 hour: € 10.00; 4 hours: € 20.00; full day: € 30.00, students (on display of a valid student card): € 22.50
OPEN > Daily, 9.00 a.m.-10.00 p.m.
INFO > Tel. +32 (0)50 33 80 27, www.bikerentalkoffieboontje.be

» Snuffel Hostel
LOCATION > Ezelstraat 42
PRICE > Full day: € 8.00
OPEN > Daily, 8.00 a.m.-8.00 p.m. (bikes have to be returned by 8.00 p.m.)
INFO > Tel. +32 (0)50 33 31 33, www.snuffel.be

» Steershop
LOCATION > Havenstraat 3
PRICE > City bike, full day: € 10.00. Racing or touring bike, full day: € 25.00; per extra day: € 15.00. Bikes must be reserved online.
OPEN > Tuesday to Saturday, 2.00 p.m.-7.00 p.m. (collecting bikes between 8.00 a.m. and 12.00 p.m. is possible following reservation online)
EXTRA > Guided tours *(see pages 155-156)*
INFO > Tel. +32 (0)474 40 84 01, www.steershop.be

Most of the bicycle rental points ask for the payment of a guarantee.

Bike taxi

A bike taxi will bring you to your destination in an ecological way.

BIKE TAXI STANDS

» Markt (near the Historium)
» 't Zand (near the Concertgebouw)
» Stationsplein (Kiss&Ride)

PRICE > Local rates are obtainable on site from the individual taxi companies.
INFO > www.taxifietsbrugge.be, www.fiets koetsenbrugge.be and www.greenrides.eu

P 🚐 Campers

The Kanaaleiland ('Canal Island') at the Bargeweg offers an excellent camping site for at least 22 camping cars all year round. Once your camper is parked, you are just a five-minute walk from the city centre (via the Beguinage). The parking area is open for new arrivals until 10.00 p.m. It is not possible to make prior reservations.
PRICE > During the period 1/4 to 30/9: € 22.50/day; during the period 1/10 to 31/3: € 15.00/day. Free electricity; it is also possible to stock up with clean water (€ 0.50) and dispose of dirty water.
INFO > www.interparking.com

Church services

01 Basiliek van het Heilig Bloed (Basilica of the Holy Blood)
Daily, except Thursday: 11.00 a.m.

02 Begijnhofkerk (Beguinage Church)
Monday to Saturday: 11.00 a.m., Sunday: 9.30 a.m.

04 English Convent
Wednesday and Friday: 7.45 a.m.

12 English Church
('t Keerske / Saint Peter's Chapel)
English language Anglican service,
Sunday: 6.00 p.m.

09 Kapel Hof Bladelin (Chapel Bladelin Court)
Sunday: 9.00 a.m.

10 Kapucijnenkerk (Capuchins Church)
Monday to Friday: 8.00 a.m. (Tuesday: also 6.00 p.m.), Saturday: 6.00 p.m., Sunday: 10.00 a.m.

11 Karmelietenkerk (Carmelites Church)
Monday to Friday: 7.00 a.m. and 6.00 p.m., Saturday: 6.00 p.m., Sunday: 10.00 a.m.

15 Onze-Lieve-Vrouwekerk (Church of Our Lady)
Saturday: 5.30 p.m., Sunday: 11.00 a.m.

16 Onze-Lieve-Vrouw-ter-Potteriekerk (Church of Our Lady of the Pottery)
Sunday: 7.00 a.m. and 9.30 a.m.

17 Onze-Lieve-Vrouw-van-Blindekens-kapel (Chapel of Our Lady of the Blind)
First Saturday of the month: 6.00 p.m.

18 Orthodoxe Kerk HH. Konstantijn & Helena (Orthodox Church Saints Constantin & Helen)
Saturday: 6.00 p.m., Sunday: 9.00 a.m.

19 Sint-Annakerk (Saint Anne's Church)
Sunday: 10.00 a.m.

20 Sint-Gilliskerk (Saint Giles's Church)
Sunday: 7.00 p.m.

22 Sint-Jakobskerk (Saint James's Church)
Wednesday and Saturday: 7.00 p.m.

23 Sint-Salvatorskathedraal (Saint Saviour's Cathedral)
Monday to Friday: 6.00 p.m. (Wednesday: also 9.00 a.m.), Saturday: 4.00 p.m., Sunday: 10.30 a.m.

12 **Verenigde Protestantse Kerk (United Protestant Church)**
('t Keerske / Saint Peter's Chapel)
Sunday: 10.00 a.m.

25 **Vrije Evangelische Kerk (Free Evangelical Church)**
Sunday: 10.00 a.m.

Cinemas

» All films are shown in their original language.

09 Cinema Liberty
Kuipersstraat 23, www.cinema-liberty.be

10 Cinema Lumière
Sint-Jakobsstraat 36, www.lumierecinema.be

11 Kinepolis Brugge
Koning Albert I-laan 200, Sint-Michiels,
www.kinepolis.com | scheduled bus no. 27,
bus stop: Kinepolis

Climate

Bruges enjoys a mild, maritime climate. The summers are warm without being hot and the winters are cold without being freezing.

During spring and autumn the temperatures are also pleasant and there is moderate rainfall throughout the year, with the heaviest concentrations in autumn and winter. So remember to bring your umbrella!

Emergencies

▶ **European emergency number**
» tel. 112. This free number is used in all member states of the European Union to contact the emergency services: police, fire brigade or medical assistance. The number operates 24 hours a day, 7 days a week.

▶ **Medical help**
» **Doctors, pharmacists, dentists and nursing officers on duty**
tel. 1733
» **Hospitals**
A.Z. St.-Jan > tel. +32 (0)50 45 21 11
A.Z. St.-Lucas > tel. +32 (0)50 36 91 11
St.-Franciscus Xaveriuskliniek >
tel. +32 (0)50 47 04 70
» **Poisons Advice Centre**
tel. +32 (0)70 245 245

▶ **Police**
» **General telephone number**
tel. +32 (0)50 44 88 44
» **Emergency police assistance**   tel. 101

» Working hours

Monday to Friday: 8.00 a.m.-5.00 p.m. and Saturday: 9.00 a.m.-6.00 p.m. you can contact the central police services at Kartuizerinnenstraat 4 | City map: E9

» After working hours

There is a 24/7 presence at the police station at the Lodewijk Coiseaukaai 3 | City map: F1

Formalities

» Identity

An identity card or valid passport is necessary. An ordinary identity card is sufficient for most citizens of the European Union. If you arrive in Belgium from outside the European Union, you must first pass through customs. There are no border controls once inside the European Union. Check at the Belgian embassy or consulate in your own country to find out exactly what documents you need.

» Health

Citizens of the European Union have access to necessary medical care through their own national health insurance card/document. This care is given under the same conditions as for the local Belgian population. You can obtain this card from your own national health service. Please note, however, that every member of the family must have his/her own card/document.

Getting there

Up-to-date information about access can be found on www.visitbruges.be

► By car/ferry

From the UK you travel to Bruges by ferry or by Eurotunnel:

» Hull (UK) – Zeebrugge (B) with P&O Ferries (crossing: 12h00). Take the N31 from Zeebrugge to Bruges. Estimated distance Zeebrugge – Bruges is 17 km or 11 miles (30 min driving).

» Dover (UK) – Dunkerque (F) with DFDS Seaways (crossing: 2h00). Take the motorway E40 to Bruges. Estimated distance Dunkerque – Bruges is 76 km or 47 miles (1h driving).

» Dover (UK) – Calais (F) with P&O Ferries or DFDS Seaways (crossing: 1h30). Estimated distance Calais – Bruges is 120 km or 75 miles (1h30 driving).

► How to get to Bruges?

departure	via	km	miles	time train ☻	time bus ☻	time boat ☻	make a reservation
Amsterdam	Brussels-South/Midi	253	157	03:12	-	-	www.thalys.com
Brussels Airport	-	110	68	01:25	-	-	www.belgianrail.be
Brussels South Charleroi Airport	-	148	92	-	02:10	-	www.flibco.com
Ostend-Bruges Airport	Oostende	24	15	See page 18		-	www.delijn.be, www.belgianrail.be
Dover	Dunkerque	-	-	-	-	02:00	www.dfdsseaways.com
Dover	Calais	-	-	-	-	01:30	www.poferries.com, www.dfdsseaways.com
Hull	Zeebrugge	-	-			1 night	www.poferries.com
Lille Flandres	Kortrijk	75	47	01:47	-	-	www.b-europe.com
London St Pancras	Brussels-South/Midi	-	-	03:25	-	-	www.eurostar.com

» **Folkestone (UK) – Calais (F)** via Eurotunnel (35 min). Estimated distance Calais – Bruges is 120 km or 75 miles (1h30 driving). **A 30 kph zone is in force throughout the entire city centre. This means that you are forbidden at all times to drive faster than 30 kilometres per hour.** Parking is for an unlimited time and is most advantageous in one of the two city centre car parks. *(For more information, see 'Parking')*

▶ By bus

Several international bus companies run frequent services to Bruges. Flibco.com operates 9 direct buses each day to and from Brussels South Charleroi Airport. On certain days, you can travel to Bruges with Flixbus from London and Dortmund (via Essen, Düsseldorf and Eindhoven). Eurolines also has daily connections to and from Bruges with London and Amsterdam (via Ghent and Utrecht). The stops for these services can all be found at the Sint-Michiels side (Spoorwegstraat) of the central train station. It is recommended to always book your seat in advance (for some companies it is obligatory).

See www.flibco.com, www.flixbus.com and www.eurolines.com for up-to-date information about arrival/departure times, fare prices and reservations.

▶ By train
» National

There are several direct train services to Bruges from the provincial capitals (Antwerp, Ghent, Hasselt and Louvain) and Brussels. Please consult www.belgianrail.be.

» International
The station at Brussel-Zuid (Brussels South) is the Belgian hub for international rail traffic. Numerous high speed trains arrive in Brussel-Zuid daily, coming from Paris (Thalys/Izy and TGV), Lille (Eurostar and TGV), London (Eurostar), Amsterdam (Thalys) and Cologne (Thalys and ICE). On weekdays, three trains leave every hour from Brussel-Zuid for Bruges, Ostend or Knokke/Blankenberge, stopping in Bruges; during the weekend, there are two trains every hour. The travelling time between Brussel-Zuid and Bruges is approximately 1 hour.

▶ By plane
» Via Brussels Airport

Each day, the national airport at Zaventem welcomes flights from more than 200 cities in 66 countries. It is easy to travel from Brussels national airport to Bruges by train. On weekdays, there is a direct hourly service. You can also take the Brussels Airport Express (four trains every hour) to Brussel-Noord (Brussels-North), Brussel-Centraal (Brussels-Central) or Brussel-Zuid (Brussels-South). On weekdays, three trains leave every hour from these stations for Ostend or Knokke/Blankenberge, stopping in Bruges; during the weekend, there are two trains every hour. Consult www.belgianrail.be for information about arrival-departure times and fare prices. For those who prefer to take a taxi, you can find all the relevant information on page 22.

» Via Brussels South Charleroi Airport
This popular regional airport receives multiple low cost flights every day from various cities and regions in Europe. The Flibco.com bus company (www.flibco.com) provides a direct shuttle bus service to and from the station in Bruges, with a frequency

of 9 trips per day (there and back). For those who prefer to take a taxi, you can find all the relevant information on page 22.

» Via Ostend-Bruges Airport

Ostend-Bruges Airport is developing rapidly and is systematically developing its range of flights and services. The railway station at Ostend is just a 15-minute bus ride away. From here, there are at least three trains to Bruges each hour between 6.00 a.m. and 10.00 p.m., with final destinations in Eupen, Welkenraedt, Brussels national airport, Antwerpen-Centraal or Kortrijk. The train journey to Bruges takes about 15 minutes. Consult www.belgianrail.be for information about arrival-departure times and fare prices. For those who prefer to take a taxi, you can find all the relevant information on page 22.

» In Bruges

From the station in Bruges, you can travel to your overnight accommodation address by bus (every five minutes; *see 'Public transport'*) or by taxi *(see 'Taxis')*.

Good to know

Don't let pickpockets ruin your shopping day. Always keep your **wallet/purse** in a closed inside pocket, and not in an open handbag or rucksack. A golden tip for ladies: always close your handbag and wear it with the fastener against your body. Bruges is a lively, fun-loving city, with great nightlife. There are plenty of places where you can amuse yourself until the early hours of the morning. Please bear in mind that it is prohibited to sell, give or serve **spirits** (whisky, gin, rum, vodka, etc.) to persons under the age of 18 years. For persons under the age of 16, this prohibition applies for all drinks with an alcohol content exceeding 0.5%. When purchasing alcohol, proof of age may be requested. All drugs – including cannabis – are prohibited by law in Belgium. Visiting Bruges means endless hours of fun, but please allow the visitors who come after you to enjoy their fun in a **clean** and **tidy** city: so always put your rubbish in a rubbish bin.

Inhabitants

On 1 January 2016, there were 19,449 inhabitants registered as living in the inner city of Bruges. The total population of Greater Bruges on the same date was 117,958.

🔒 Lockers

» Station (railway station)
Stationsplein | City map: C13

» **30** Historium
Markt 1

Market days

» Monday
8.00 a.m.-1.30 p.m. | Onder de Toren – Lissewege | miscellaneous
» Wednesday
8.00 a.m.-1.30 p.m. | Markt | food and flowers
» Friday
8.00 a.m.-1.30 p.m. | Market Square – Zeebrugge | miscellaneous
» Saturday
8.00 a.m.-1.30 p.m. | 't Zand and Beursplein | miscellaneous

» Sunday
7.00 a.m.-2.00 p.m. | Veemarkt, Sint-Michiels | miscellaneous
» Wednesday to Saturday
8.00 a.m.-1.30 p.m. | Vismarkt | fish
» Daily
8.00 a.m.-7.00 p.m. | Vismarkt | artisanal products
» Saturday, Sunday, public holidays and bridge days in the period 15/3 to 15/11 + also on Friday in the period June to September
10.00 a.m.-6.00 p.m. | Dijver | antique, bric-à-brac and crafts

Money

Most of the banks in Bruges are open from 9.00 a.m. to 12.30 p.m. and from 2.00 p.m. to 4.30 p.m. Many branch offices are also open on Saturday morning, but on Sunday they are all closed. There are cash points ⛟ in several shopping streets, on 't Zand, Simon Stevinplein, Stationsplein (Railway station Square) and on Bargeplein. You can easily withdraw money from cash machines with Visa, Eurocard or MasterCard. Currency can be exchanged in every bank or in an exchange office. In the event of the loss or theft of your bank or credit card, it is best to immediately block the card by calling Card Stop on tel. 070 344 344 (24 hours a day).
» Exchange office Goffin Change nv
OPEN > Monday to Saturday, 9.00 a.m.-6.00 p.m.
INFO > Steenstraat 2 | City map: E8
» Exchange office Pillen bvba
OPEN > Monday to Friday, 9.00 a.m.-12.30 p.m. and 1.30 p.m.-4.45 p.m.; Saturday, 9.00 a.m.-12.30 p.m. and 2.00 p.m.-4.00 p.m.
INFO > Vlamingstraat 18 | City map: E7
» Exchange office Pillen R.W.J. bvba
OPEN > Thursday to Tuesday, 10.00 a.m.-5.30 p.m.; Wednesday, 10.00 a.m.-5.00 p.m.
INFO > Rozenhoedkaai 2 | City map: F8

Opening hours

Cafés and restaurants have no (fixed) closing hour. Sometimes they will remain open until the early hours of the morning and other days they will close earlier: it all depends on the number of customers. *(See 'Shopping in Bruges' for info about shop opening times, page 27)*

Parking

Bruges is a city on a human scale. The use of motor vehicles in the historic inner city is not recommended and street parking above ground is limited in time to a maximum of 4 hours in the Blue Zone and to 2 hours in the Pay&Display Zones. From 16/02/2017 paid car parking will be applicable everywhere in the city centre, from 9.00 a.m. to 8.00 p.m. You can easily park your car in one of the underground car parks, which is usually less expensive. Parking for an unlimited time is cheapest in one of the two city centre car parks: at the front side (City map: D13) of the station or under 't Zand. Both are situated within walking distance of the city centre, but you can also use the bus transfer with De Lijn *(read more under the section 'Public transport')* between the parking Centrum-Station and the city centre (included in your parking fee for 4 passengers). The Park and Ride areas are situated right outside of the city centre. Here you can park your car for free and for a longer duration. The city centre is a stone's throw away on foot or by bus. If you are staying in Bruges, ask in advance for information about possible parking options at or near your overnight accommodation.
» Info
Consult www.visitbruges.be for more information about car parking in Bruges.

▶ Parking Centrum-Station
Stationsplein | City map: D13
CAPACITY > 1500
OPEN > Daily, 24 hours a day

PRICE > Maximum € 3.50/24 hrs | hourly rate: € 0.70 | including free bus transfer (max. 4 persons per car)

▶ Parking Centrum-'t Zand
onder 't Zand | City map: C9
CAPACITY > 1400
OPEN > Daily, 24 hours a day
PRICE > Maximum € 8.70/24 hrs | hourly rate: € 1.20; from the second hour you pay per quarter hour

Post offices
» bpost Smedenstraat
Smedenstraat 57-59 | City map: B9
For posting letters, cards, etc. and for the purchase of stamps you can go to one of the postal points or stamp shops that you will find in various shopping streets throughout the city.

Public holidays
Belgium has quite a lot of public holidays. On these holidays most companies, shops, offices and public services are closed.
» 1 January (New Year's Day)
» 16 April (Easter Sunday)
  and 17 April (Easter Monday)
» 1 May (Labour Day)
» 25 May (Ascension Day)
» 4 June (Whit Sunday)
  and 5 June (Whit Monday)
» 11 July (Flemish regional holiday)
» 21 July (Belgian national holiday)
» 15 August (Assumption of Mary)
» 1 November (All Saints' Day)
» 11 November (Armistice Day)
» 25 December (Christmas)
» 26 December (Boxing Day)

Public transport
▶ 🚌 Bus
Public transport in Bruges is well organized. Buses run every five minutes between the station and the city centre. There are

also frequent services to the station and the city centre running from the bus stop for tourist buses at the Kanaaleiland ('canal Island'; City map: E13). The buses going to the city centre stop within easy walking distance of the main shopping streets, historical buildings and museums. The most important bus stops are marked on the city map (see the folding map on the inside of the back cover). A ticket allows you to change bus services as many times as you want for a period of 60 minutes. The ticket price is € 3.00. All De Lijn tickets can be bought at the following points of sale.

▶ Tickets
» Advance sales offices
De Lijnwinkel, Stationsplein
ℹ️ Tourist office on 't Zand (Concertgebouw)
Various book stores, newsagents and supermarkets in the city centre
» Vending machines De Lijn
De Lijnwinkel, Stationsplein
Bus stop 't Zand
» Info
You can find the most up-to-date travel information on www.visitbruges.be

Scooter rental
» 🛵 Electric Scooters
Rental of electric scooters
(max. speed: 25 kph).
LOCATION > Gentpoortstraat 55 and 62
PRICE PER SCOOTER > 2 hours: € 35.00; 4 hours: € 50.00; full day: € 65.00

OPEN > During the period 1/4 to 31/10: Wednesday to Saturday, 10.00 a.m.-6.00 p.m.
CONDITIONS > Minimum driver age = 23 years
EXTRA > Rental of electric bikes (see page 13)
INFO > Tel. +32 (0)474 09 19 18, www.electric-scooters.be

» 🛵 Vespa Tours
LOCATION > Estaminet 't Molenhuis, Potterierei 109
PRICE PER VESPA > Including helmet and insurance, half day: € 50.00 (1 person) or € 65.00 (2 persons); full day: € 70.00 (1 person) or € 80.00 (2 persons)
OPEN > During the period 1/3 to 31/10: daily, 10.00 a.m.-6.00 p.m.
CONDITIONS > Minimum driver age = 21 years, driver's license B
EXTRA > Guided tours (see page 157)
INFO > Tel. +32 (0)497 64 86 48, www.vespatours-brugge.be

» 🛵 Vesparoute.com
LOCATION > Fietsverhuur B-Bike, Concertgebouw, 't Zand
PRICE PER VESPA > Including helmet, insurance and petrol, half day: € 50.00 (1 person) or € 60.00 (2 persons), not possible on Saturday and Sunday; full day: € 79.00 (1 person) or € 89.00 (2 persons)
OPEN > During the period 15/3 to 31/10: daily, 10.00 a.m.-6.00 p.m.
CONDITIONS > Minimum age driver = 21 years, driver's license B
INFO > Tel. +32 (0)479 97 12 80 or +32 (0)474 55 34 45, www.vesparoute.com

The hirers of scooters usually ask for the payment of a security deposit before departure.

Smoking

In Belgium there is a general ban on smoking in cafés, restaurants, the public areas in hotels (lobby, bar, corridors, etc.) and in all public buildings (train stations, airports, etc.). Those unable to kick the habit will usually find an ashtray just outside (often under shelter).

Swimming pools

11 Interbad
Six 25-meter lanes; also a recreational pool, water slide, toddler's pool and teaching pool.
INFO > Veltemweg 35, Sint-Kruis, tel. +32 (0)50 35 07 77, interbad@skynet.be, www.interbad.be; scheduled bus no. 10, no. 58 or no. 58S, bus stop: Watertoren

12 Jan Guilini
25-meter indoor pool in a beautiful listed building, named after the swimming champion and resistance fighter Jan Guilini.
INFO > Keizer Karelstraat 41, tel. +32 (0)50 31 35 54, zwembadjanguilini@brugge.be, www.brugge.be/sport; scheduled bus no. 9, bus stop: Visartpark

13 🛜 S&R Olympia
In addition to a 50-meter olympic sports pool, S&R Olympia offers extensive recreational facilities in the 'sub-tropical swimming paradise'. In fine weather, you can use the large lawn with its two outdoor pools and various other attractions.
INFO > Doornstraat 110, Sint-Andries, tel. +32 (0)50 67 28 70, olympia@sr-olympia.be, www.sr-olympia.be; scheduled bus no. 5, bus stop: Lange Molen or no. 25, bus stop: Jan Breydel

All information about opening times is available at the 🛈 tourist office Markt (Historium), 't Zand (Concertgebouw) or Stationsplein (Station, railway station).

Taxis

🚕 TAXI STANDS

» At Bruges station: city centre side and Sint-Michiels side
» At the Bargeweg (Kanaaleiland)
» On the Markt
» In the Vlamingstraat (opposite the City Theatre)
» In the Boeveriestraat (near 't Zand)

PRICE > The local taxi companies all use the same fixed rate tariffs (adjustments are possible throughout the year):

Bruges <> Brussels Airport: € 200.00
Bruges <> Brussels South Charleroi Airport: € 250.00
Bruges <> Aéroport de Lille: € 140.00
Bruges <> Ostend-Bruges Airport: € 70.00
Bruges <> Brussels (city centre): € 175.00
Bruges <> Zeebrugge: € 50.00

A list of the licensed taxi-cab firms can be found on www.visitbruges.be. By using the handy free app PickMeUp (available in the App Store and on Google Play), you can quickly find the nearest available licensed taxi in your area.

Telephoning

If you want to phone someone in Bruges from abroad, you must first dial the country code (00)32, followed by the zone code 50, and the number of the person you want. To phone Bruges from inside Belgium, you dial 050 plus the number of the person.

Toilets

There are a number of public toilets wc in Bruges (see the fold-out plan at the back of the guide). Some are accessible for wheelchair users. You will also find (free) toilets in some of the larger department stores. When local people need the toilet, they often pop into a cafe or pub to order something small so that they can use the facilities there.

ℹ 🛜 ♿ Tourist offices

There are three tourist information offices in Bruges: one in the Historium (Market Square), one in the Concertgebouw (Concert Hall) and a third in the railway station.

» **Tourist office Market Square (Historium)**
Daily, 10.00 a.m.-5.00 p.m.
» **Tourist office 't Zand (Concertgebouw)**
Monday to Saturday, 10.00 a.m.-5.00 p.m.; Sunday and public holidays, 10.00 a.m.-2.00 p.m.
» **Tourist office Railway Station (platform's corridor, city centre side)**
Daily, 10.00 a.m.-5.00 p.m.

All tourist offices are closed on Christmas Day and New Year's Day. Tel. +32 (0)50 44 46 46, toerisme@brugge.be, www.visitbruges.be

Travelling season

Although most visitors come to the city in the spring and summer months, Bruges has something to offer all year round. The misty months of autumn and winter are ideal for atmospheric strolls along the canals and the cobbled streets, before ending up in a cosy restaurant or cheerful pub. The 'cold' months are also perfect for undisturbed visits to the city's many museums and sites of interest, before again finishing up in one of those same restaurants or pubs! What's more, in January, February and March you can get great discounts on many accommodation outlets in Bruges.

Bruges for bon-vivants

Bruges is a paradise for food connoisseurs. Its culinary delights range from Michelin-star establishments of international quality and reputation, through stylish local bistros and brasseries, to traditional Italian or Asian specialty restaurants.

Award winning restaurants

Bruges is one of the gastronomic centres of Europe and boasts an impressive number of star-rated restaurants. Whether you swear by fish or prefer meat; whether you love beer in your dishes or would rather have a wine-based sauce; whether you are a fan of exotic culinary delights or a devotee of authentic, local cooking, the superior kitchens in Bruges have so much to offer that everyone will be able to discover a recipe to his or her taste.

» **De Jonkman**   Maalse Steenweg 438, 8310 Sint-Kruis, tel. +32 (0)50 36 07 67, www.dejonkman.be (2 Michelin-stars, 18/20 graded by GaultMillau)
» **Den Gouden Harynck**   Groeninge 25, 8000 Brugge, tel. +32 (0)50 33 76 37, www.goudenharynck.be (1 Michelin-star, 17/20 graded by GaultMillau)
» **Sans Cravate**   Langestraat 159, 8000 Brugge, tel. +32 (0)50 67 83 10, www.sanscravate.be (1 Michelin-star, 16/20 graded by GaultMillau)

» **Auberge De Herborist**   De Watermolen 15, 8200 Sint-Andries,
tel. +32 (0)50 38 76 00, www.aubergedeherborist.be (1 Michelin-star,
15/20 graded by GaultMillau)

» **A'Qi**   Gistelse Steenweg 686, 8200 Sint-Andries, tel. +32 (0)50 30 05 99 or
+32 (0)470 97 04 55, www.restaurantaqi.be (1 Michelin-star, 15/20 graded
by GaultMillau)

» **Bistro Bruut**   Meestraat 9, 8000 Brugge, tel. +32 (0)50 69 55 09,
www.bistrobruut.be (15/20 graded by GaultMillau)

» **Goffin**   Maalse Steenweg 2, 8310 Sint-Kruis, tel. +32 (0)50 68 77 88,
www.timothygoffin.be (15/20 graded by GaultMillau)

» **L.E.S.S.**   Torhoutse Steenweg 479, 8200 Sint-Michiels, tel. +32 (0)50 69 93 69,
www.l-e-s-s.be (15/20 graded by GaultMillau)

» **Patrick Devos**   Zilverstraat 41, 8000 Brugge, tel. +32 (0)50 33 55 66,
www.patrickdevos.be (15/20 graded by GaultMillau)

» **Rock-Fort**   Langestraat 15-17, 8000 Brugge, tel. +32 (0)50 33 41 13,
www.rock-fort.be (15/20 graded by GaultMillau)

» **Bistro Refter**   Molenmeers 2, 8000 Brugge, tel. +32 (0)50 44 49 00,
www.bistrorefter.be (14/20 graded by GaultMillau and selected
as Bib Gourmand)

» **bonte B**   Dweersstraat 12, 8000 Brugge, tel. +32 (0)50 34 83 43,
www.restaurantbonteb.be (14/20 graded by GaultMillau)

» **Floris**   Gistelse Steenweg 520, 8200 Sint-Andries, tel. +32 (0)50 73 60 20,
www.florisrestaurant.be (14/20 graded by GaultMillau)

» **Hubert Gastrobar**   Langestraat 155-159, 8000 Brugge, tel. +32 (0)50 64 10 09
(14/20 graded by GaultMillau)

» **La Tâche**   Blankenbergse Steenweg 1, 8000 Sint-Pieters, tel. +32 (0)50 68 02 52,
www.latache.be (14/20 graded by GaultMillau)

» **Le Mystique**   Niklaas Desparsstraat 11, 8000 Brugge, tel. +32 (0)50 44 44 45,
www.lemystique.be (14/20 graded by GaultMillau)

» **'t Pandreitje**   Pandreitje 6, 8000 Brugge, tel. +32 (0)50 33 11 90,
www.pandreitje.be (14/20 graded by GaultMillau)

» **Tanuki**   Oude Gentweg 1, 8000 Brugge, tel. +32 (0)50 34 75 12,
www.tanuki.be (14/20 graded by GaultMillau)

» **Tête Pressée**   Koningin Astridlaan 100, 8200 Sint-Michiels, tel. +32 (0)470 21 26 27,
www.tetepressee.be (14/20 graded by GaultMillau)

» **Assiette Blanche**   Philipstockstraat 23-25, 8000 Brugge, tel. +32 (0)50 34 00 94,
www.assietteblanche.be (13/20 graded by GaultMillau and selected
as Bib Gourmand)

» **Bhavani**   Simon Stevinplein 5, 8000 Brugge, tel. +32 (0)50 33 90 25,
www.bhavani.be (13/20 graded by GaultMillau)

» **De Mangerie**   Oude Burg 20, 8000 Brugge, tel. +32 (0)50 33 93 36,
www.mangerie.com (13/20 graded by GaultMillau)

» **Kok au Vin**   Ezelstraat 21, 8000 Brugge, tel. +32 (0)50 33 95 21,
www.kok-au-vin.be (13/20 graded by GaultMillau and selected as Bib Gourmand)

» **Lieven**   Philipstockstraat 45, 8000 Brugge, tel. +32 (0)50 68 09 75,
www.etenbijlieven.be (13/20 graded by GaultMillau)

» **'t Zwaantje**   Gentpoortvest 70, 8000 Brugge, tel. +32 (0)473 71 25 80,
» www.hetzwaantje.be (13/20 graded by GaultMillau)

» **Bistro Rombaux**   Moerkerkse Steenweg 139, 8310 Sint-Kruis,
tel. +32 (0)50 73 79 49,www.bistrorombaux.be (recommended by GaultMillau)

» **De Florentijnen**   Academiestraat 1, 8000 Brugge, tel. +32 (0)50 67 75 33,
www.deflorentijnen.be (recommended by GaultMillau)

» **De Visscherie**   Vismarkt 8, 8000 Brugge, tel. +32 (0)50 33 02 12,
www.visscherie.be (recommended by GaultMillau)

» **Duc de Bourgogne**   Huidenvettersplein 12, 8000 Brugge, tel. +32 (0)50 33 20 38,
www.ducdebourgogne.be (recommended by GaultMillau)

» **Huyze Die Maene**   Markt 17, 8000 Brugge, tel. +32 (0)50 33 39 59,
www.huyzediemaene.be (recommended by GaultMillau)

» **'t Jong Gerecht**   Langestraat 119, 8000 Brugge, tel. +32 (0)50 31 32 32,
www.tjonggerecht.be (recommended by GaultMillau)

» **Kwizien Divien**   Hallestraat 4, 8000 Brugge, tel. +32 (0)50 34 71 29,
www.kwiziendivien.be (recommended by GaultMillau)

» **Parkrestaurant**   Minderbroedersstraat 1, 8000 Brugge, tel. +32 (0)497 80 18 72,
www.parkrestaurant.be (recommended by GaultMillau)

» **The Blue Lobster**   Tijdokstraat 9, 8380 Zeebrugge, tel. +32 (0)50 68 45 71,
www.thebluelobster.be (recommended by GaultMillau)

» **'t Apertje**   Damse Vaart-Zuid 223, 8310 Sint-Kruis, tel. +32 (0)50 35 00 12,
www.apertje.be (selected as Bib Gourmand)

» **Kurt's Pan**   Sint-Jakobsstraat 58, 8000 Brugge, tel. +32 (0)50 34 12 24,
www.kurtspan.be (selected as Bib Gourmand)

More tips on finding the right address for you can be found in the section 'Tips from Bruges
experts'. Pages 108-109, 116-117, 124-125, 132-133, 140-141

Shopping in Bruges

Bruges has lots of shops to offer you something special: authentic places that surprise you again and again with their clever and original products. The city is rightly famous for its harmonious mix of creative and trendy newcomers, vintage addresses where nostalgia rules, and classic establishments that have been run with success for decades by

Where to shop?

Because Bruges is pedestrian-friendly and the main streets are all close to each other, a day's shopping here is much more relaxing than in many other cities. You will find all the major national and international chains, as well as trendy local boutiques. And if you leave the beaten shopping paths you will certainly make plenty of interesting new discoveries. The most important shopping streets (indicated in yellow on the removable city map) run between the Market Square and the old city gates: Steenstraat, Simon Stevinplein, Mariastraat, Zuidzandstraat, Sint-Jakobsstraat, Sint-Amandsstraat, Geldmuntstraat, Noordzandstraat, Smedenstraat, Vlamingstraat, Academiestraat, Philipstockstraat, Hoogstraat, Langestraat and Katelijnestraat. There is also a small but elegant shopping centre, the Zilverpand, hidden between Noordzandstraat and Zuidzandstraat. Each neighbourhood has its own unique atmosphere. In Steenstraat, for example, you will find the famous brand names, whereas Langestraat boasts many little secondhand and bric-à-brac shops. The large hypermarkets are located just outside the city centre.

When to shop?

Most shops operate from Monday to Saturday, opening at 10.00 a.m. and closing at either 6.00 or 6.30 p.m. But this does not mean that you need to go home empty-handed if you come to Bruges on a Sunday. Many specialist stores are open on Sunday as well. And on 'Shopping Sundays' – the first Sunday of the month, except on public holidays, from 1.00 p.m. to 6.00 p.m. – they are joined by the majority of the other shops. To make your shopping experience more pleasant, there is restricted access for traffic on Saturdays and 'Shopping Sundays' in the following shopping streets: Zuidzandstraat, Steenstraat, Geldmuntstraat and Noordzandstraat (from 1.00 p.m. to 6.00 p.m.).

Bruges' craftspersons and specialty stores

Creativity is built into the DNA of the people of Bruges; so it should come as no surprise to anyone that nowadays the city is teeming with innovative entrepreneurs. In the charming craft shops you are guaranteed to find an original, handmade gift to surprise your family and friends back home. Surf to www.handmadeinbrugge.be and discover dozens of fun addresses and inspiring stories. Also check out the official city app Xplore Bruges, which will take you to all the

city's 'hearths of creativity', both old and new. Feeling a little bit lost with all this choice? On www.visitbruges.be you can find a selection of the very best shopping locations in Bruges city centre: a mix of authentic shops offering products that are made in Bruges and renowned specialty stores that have already been focusing on a single product (line) for more than 25 years.

Off to the market

There is nothing quite as delightful as shopping at a local market. In Bruges, this is possible almost every day. On Wednesday there is a food market on the Market Square (8.00 a.m. to 1.30 p.m.). On Saturday (8.00 a.m.-1.30 p.m.) the Zand Square and the Beursplein are taken over by a large food and general market (flowers, animals, clothing, etc.). And on Sunday, from 7.00 a.m. to 2.00 p.m., you can visit the food and general market on the Veemarkt, near the Koningin Astridlaan in the Sint-Michiels district. Every morning (8.00 a.m.- 1.30 p.m.) from Wednesday to Saturday, you can buy fresh fish and fish dishes at the Vismarkt (Fish Market). Finally, during the weekends and on public holidays from mid-March to mid-November, you can browse at the second-hand and craft market along the Dijver (10.00 a.m.-6.00 p.m.). If you love old bric-à-brac and antiques, you should definitely visit the 'Zandfeesten', the largest secondhand and craft market in Belgium, which is organized three times

each summer (in early July, early August and late September) on the Zand Square and in the Koning Albertpark *(also see pages 18-19 and 98-100)*.

Typical Bruges souvenirs

Bruges was a flourishing centre of the diamond trade as early as the 14th century, and the city also boasted a number of professional diamond-cutting establishments. In the diamond laboratory of the Bruges Diamond Museum, you will learn how all that sparkling splendour is assessed and processed. You might even find some glittering ideas for a little investment of your own! After that, it's only a matter of checking out the museum shop or the many other jewellery stores in the city with a keen connoisseur's eye before making your move – and cashing in! *You can find more information about the Bruges Diamond Museum on pages 81-82.*

Since time immemorial, lace has also been inextricably connected to Bruges. Once upon a time, as many as a quarter of all the women in the city were employed making lace. Nowadays, you can

Brugsch Swaentje

still see female lace-makers in action in several of the Bruges lace shops. *You can find more information about lace and the Lace Centre on page 85 and in the interview with Kumiko Nakazaki on pages 128-131.*

The people of Bruges have always liked a glass or two of good beer. Especially local beer. The city can boast several excellent locally made ales – *Straffe Hendrik* and *Brugse Zot*, both brewed by De Halve Maan Brewery, right in the heart of the historic city centre – as well as four tradi-tional-style beers, including the *Fort Lapin 8 Triple* and the *Fort Lapin 10*

Quadruple, both brewed in the Fort Lapin Brewery on the edge of the city, and the *Bourgogne des Flanders*, which you can sample in the brewery of the same name along the Dijver. Have we convinced you? Then why not visit the annual Bruges Beer Festival or the Bruges Beer Muse-um on the Markt. *You can find more infor-mation about the Halve Maan and Bour-gogne des Flandres breweries and the Bruges Beer Museum on pages 77-79; more information about the Bruges Beer Festival on page 96.*

Perhaps you are not such a fan of beer? Those with a sweet tooth can visit one of the more than 50 chocolate bou-tiques that cater to all tastes: from deli-ciously old-fashioned chocolate blocks, through finger-licking good pralines that melt in your mouth, to ingenious molecular chocolate preparations tai-lored to the requirements of the city's star chefs. *Read more about chocolate on pages 79-80.*

Spinolarei and
Jan van Eyckplein

Walking in
Bruges

Walk 1
Bruges,
proud World Heritage City

Bruges may be, quite rightly, very proud of her World Heritage status, but the city is happily embracing the future too! This walk takes you along world-famous panoramic views, sky-high monuments and centuries-old squares invigorated by contemporary constructions. One foot planted in the Middle Ages, the other one firmly planted in the present. This walk is an absolute must for first-time visitors who would like to explore the very heart of the city straight away. Keep your camera at the ready!

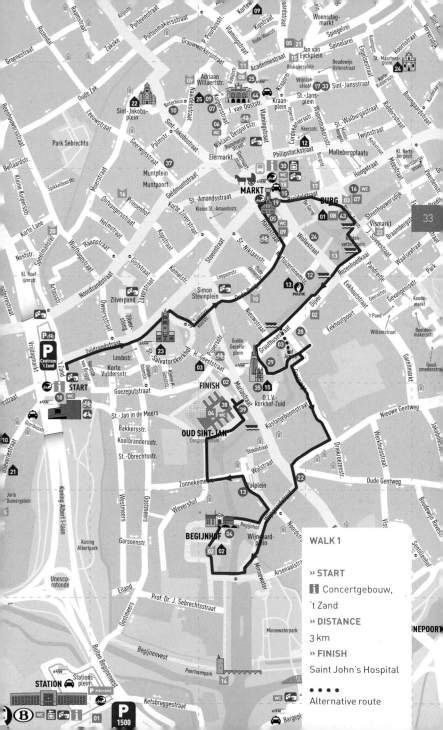

WALK 1

» START
Concertgebouw,
't Zand

» DISTANCE
3 km

» FINISH
Saint John's Hospital

• • • •
Alternative route

From 't Zand to Simon Stevinplein

This walk starts at the ℹ tourist office 't Zand (Concertgebouw).

't Zand is dominated by the Concert Hall **18**, one of Bruges' most talked-about buildings. Clear-cut proof that this World Heritage city isn't afraid of the future. As of September 2017 the Concert Hall – Open House **18** will take you behind the scenes and right to the very top of this magnificent building, where you can find an interactive space for sound art. You can also enjoy the wonderful view over the Bruges skyline. Don't forget to drop in at the ℹ tourist office 't Zand (Concertgebouw) on the ground floor: here you will find all the necessary tourist information as well as expert advice on all cultural events.

Leave ℹ 't Zand (Concertgebouw) behind you, walk along the square and turn into Zuidzandstraat, the first street on the right. Saint Saviour's Cathedral **23** looms up ahead on your right after three hundred metres. Bruges' oldest parish church is located on a lower level than the present Zuidzandstraat, which is situated on an old sand ridge. What's more, in the Middle Ages people simply threw their refuse out onto the street where it was then flattened by passing carts and coaches. This raised the street level even further. Inside Saint Saviour's, the church tower's wooden rafters can be lit. The cathedral treasury displays interesting copper memorial plaques, fine examples of gold and silver and paintings by Dieric Bouts, Hugo van der Goes and Pieter Pourbus.

Continue past the cathedral and walk down Sint-Salvatorskerkhof immediately on the right. Turn left

into Sint-Salvatorskoorstraat. The Simon Stevinplein opens up at the end of this street.

This attractive square, lined with cosy restaurant terraces in summertime, is named after Simon Stevin, a wellknown Flemish-Dutch scientist. His gracious statue naturally takes centre stage.

Markt and Burg

Continue down Oude Burg, a street in the right-hand corner of the square. Before long you will see the Cloth Halls **09** on your left. These belong to the Belfry **05**. You're allowed to cross the halls' imposing inner court between 8.00 a.m. and 6.00 p.m. during the week, and between 9.00 a.m. and 6.00 p.m. on Saturday. The Markt is at the other end of the yard. If the gate is closed, turn back and walk down Hallestraat, which runs parallel to the Halls.

Walk 2 (see pages 45-47) comments more extensively on Markt.

Return to the Belfry **05** and walk down Breidelstraat, a traffic-free alley on the corner at the left. Continue to the Burg square.

Along the way on your right you will notice De Garre, a narrow alley. This may be the narrowest street in Bruges (try walking side by side here!), it nevertheless boasts a fair number of cosy cafés. The Burg is the most majestic square in the city, so take your time to admire its grandeur. The main character in this medieval story is the City Hall **08** **43** (1376-1420), one of the oldest city halls in the Netherlands and a Gothic example for all its brothers and sisters that were built later, from Louvain to Audenarde and Brussels. Having admired its exterior, enter the impressive Gothic Hall and gaze in admiration at the polychrome floating ribs of the vaulted ceiling. Hiding on the right-hand side of this Gothic monument is the Basilica of the Holy Blood **01**. It was originally dedicated to both Our Lady and Saint

BURG SQUARE: AN ARCHITECTURAL SYNOPSIS

Art lovers have already noticed that the Burg projects a wonderful cross-section of stunning architectural styles. It is, indeed, a summing-up in one place of all the styles that have caught our imagination throughout the various centuries. From Romanesque (Saint Basil's Church) and Gothic (City Hall) by way of Renaissance (Civil Registry) and Baroque (Deanery) to Classicism (Mansion of the Liberty of Bruges). There's no need to go and dash all around Bruges to see it all!

01

Basil, and was built as a fortress church on two levels between 1139 and 1157. The lower church, hidden away behind the Gothic Saint Ivo's Chapel, has retained its Romanesque character. The upper chapel, which was originally little more than a kind of balcony, was gradually extended over the years to become a church in its own right. It was only during the 19th century that it was renovated in the neo-Gothic style that can be seen today. The sacred relic of the Holy Blood has been kept here since the 13th century. In a tradition dating back to at least 1304, each year on Ascension Day the relic is carried in the Holy Blood Procession, a popular event that captures the imagination of the entire city. Facing the basilica is the gleaming Renaissance façade of the erstwhile Civil Registry 03 (1534-1537, which now houses the City Archive 07) adjacent to the Liberty of Bruges 16. Its showpiece is a splendid oak mantelpiece with an alabaster frieze (1529). From the adjoining Palace of the Liberty of Bruges (with its facade dating from 1722), the countryside in a wide area

around the city was once governed. After 1795, the building became a courtroom and since 1988 it has housed various branches of the city administration. Once upon a time Saint Donatian's Cathedral graced the spot directly in front of the City Hall. The church was torn down in 1799. Adjacent to it is the Deanery 17 (1655-1666). It is still possible to see parts of the old cathedral in the cellar of the Crown Plaza Hotel.

Fishy stories

Proceed to Blinde-Ezelstraat, the little street to the left of the City Hall. Don't forget to look back at the lovely arch between the City Hall and the Old Civil Registry 03 07. Do you see Solomon? Left of him is the statue of Prosperity, to the right the statue of Peace.

According to tradition, Blinde-Ezelstraat (Blind Donkey Street) owes its name to a tavern of the same name. In olden days, the breweries that delivered beer to the taverns in the city used donkeys to turn their treadmills. To stop the poor beasts from realizing that they were just going around in circles, they were fitted with a blindfold. From the bridge, a few metres further along on the left, you can see the Meebrug, one of the oldest bridges in the city.

Vismarkt 22 opens up immediately past the bridge.

Originally, fish was sold on the corner of the main market square, where the Historium 30 now stands, but the fish sellers were later forced to move here

because of the smell. In the covered arcade, specially erected for the purpose in 1821, fresh seafood was sold, a delicacy that only the rich could afford. Today you can still buy your fresh saltwater fish here every morning from Wednesday to Saturday. In summer, the Fish Market is also regularly used as the atmospheric setting for music and dance events.

Retrace your steps and turn left in front of the bridge towards Huidenvettersplein.
Whereas Vismarkt served the rich, Huidenvettersplein (Tanners Square)

served the poor. No sea fish on the menu here, but affordable freshwater fish. The post in the middle of the square used to have a twin brother: in between the two posts hung the scales that the fish were weighed on. The large, striking building dominating the square used to be the meeting hall of the tanners. Here they sold the cow hides that they had turned into leather. Since tanning was a rather smelly job, it is no coincidence that the tanners' hall adjoined the fish market. Look out for the statuette adorning the corner of the hall. It is no surprise that the little fellow raises his nose.

Continue to Rozenhoedkaai. Keep right. Rozenhoedkaai is the most photographed spot in Bruges. So, take out your camera! This was once the place where the salt traders loaded and unloaded their goods. Salt was the gold of the Middle Ages: you could use it both to preserve food and to give added flavour to your cooking. Its value is underlined by the fact that the origin of the modern

Huidenvettersplein

word *salary* comes from the Latin word *sal*, which means 'salt'. Roman soldiers used to be paid in salt.

From Groeninge to the Bonifacius Bridge

Continue along Dijver.

In the middle of the 11th century, the hermit Everelmus built a prayer chapel on Dijver. Along this atmospheric stretch of water, you will first find the College of Europe (numbers 9 to 11) **02**, an international postgraduate institution that focuses on European affairs, and then the Groeninge Museum (number 12) **28**, Bruges' most renowned museum. On display are world-famous masterpieces by Jan van Eyck, Hans Memling, Hugo van der Goes, Gerard David and many other Flemish primitives. The museum also has a valuable collection of Flemish expressionists, neoclassical top notch paintings from the 18th and 19th centuries and post-war modern art. Overall, the museum shows a complete overview of Belgian and southern Dutch (Flemish) painting from the 15th to the 20th century. The museum entrance is reached through a few picturesque courtyard gardens.

Would you like to find out more about the Flemish primitives? Then leaf through to the interview on pages 112-115 with Till-Holger Borchert, the Groeninge Museum's chief curator.

Continue along Dijver. The entrance gate to the Gruuthuse Museum **29** is on your left just beyond the little bridge. This museum is closed for restoration until 2018.

ALMSHOUSES, THE QUICKEST WAY TO HEAVEN

These charitable dwellings were built from the 14th century onwards. Sometimes by the trade guilds, who wanted to offer their ageing members a roof over their heads; sometimes by widows or wealthy citizens, who hoped to secure their place in heaven with a display of Christian charity.

In order to secure their spot, each set of almshouses had its own chapel, in which the inhabitants were morally obliged to offer prayers of thanks to heaven. Practically all of the almshouses have been carefully restored and modernised and offer cosy living to today's elderly, whilst their small yet picturesque gardens and white-painted façades offer welcoming peace and quiet to the present-day visitor. Feel free to enter these premises, but don't forget to respect their perfect tranquillity. *(On the City map the Almshouses are indicated by* 🏠*.)*

Bonifacius Bridge

(28)

Continue to Guido Gezelleplein, then turn left in front of the Church of Our Lady (15) (35) and follow the narrow footpath to the picturesque Bonifacius Bridge. Due to renovation works, it is possible that the footpath will be closed for a time. If this is the case, follow the alternative route as indicated on the map (dotted line).

The crosses that you see all over the place don't belong to graves at all – they are crosses taken down from church steeples during the First World War to disorientate the enemy spies. The crosses have never been put up again. Close to the Bonifacius Bridge is Bruges' smallest Gothic window. Look up! It was through this window that the lords and ladies of Gruuthuse were able to peer down onto their private jetty. Across the bridge is the charming city garden Hof Arents of the Arentshuis (03), an elegant 17th-century abode. The top floor houses work by the versatile British artist Frank Brangwyn. The ground floor is reserved for temporary exhibitions. The garden contains a remarkable group of statues by Rik Poot (1924-2006) depicting the *Four Horse-men of the Apocalypse*, who represent revolution, war, hunger and death. This religious theme also fascinated Hans Memling, since the Horsemen are also present in his *St. John Triptych*, which can be seen in the nearby St. John's Hospital (39). The garden gate leads through to the Groeninge Museum, (28) where you can admire more works by Memling and his contemporaries.

On to the Beguinage!

Leave the garden once more through the narrow garden gate and turn left into Groeninge, a winding street. Turn right again at the intersection with Nieuwe Gentweg. Notice the Saint Joseph and the De Meulenaere almshouses (both from the 17th century). Continue down the street. On the left-hand corner of Oude Gent-weg and Katelijnestraat is the Diamond Museum (22), Bruges' most glittering museum and the place to be for all lovers of bling. It goes without saying that an inspiring diamond museum simply couldn't be absent in the most romantic city of the western hemisphere!

Wijngaardplein

Turn left into Katelijnestraat, then immediately right into Wijngaardstraat. Cross Wijngaardplein – a stopping place for coachmen. A little further on turn right onto the bridge beside the Sashuis (lock house) to enter the Beguinage. The bridge offers a fine view of the Minnewater.

The Minnewater used to be the landing stage of the barges or track boats that provided a regular connection between Bruges and Ghent. Today it is one of Bruges' most romantic beauty spots. Equally atmospheric, yet of a totally different nature, is the Beguinage. Although the 'Princely Beguinage Ten Wijngaarde' **02** **02**, founded in 1245, is no longer occupied by beguines (devout and celibate women who formed a religious community without taking holy orders), but by nuns of the Order of St. Benedict and a number of unmarried Bruges women, you can still form an excellent picture of what daily life looked like in the 17th century at the Beguine's house **04**. The imposing courtyard garden, the white painted house fronts and blessed peace create an atmosphere all of its own. The entrance gates are closed each day at 6.30 p.m. without fail.

Walk around the Beguinage and leave through the main gate. Turn left after the bridge and left again to reach Walplein.

De Halve Maan **13**, a brewery established as early as 1564, is at number 26 (on your left hand side). This is Bruges' oldest active city brewery. Their speciality is *Brugse Zot* (Bruges' Fool), a spirited top-fermented beer made from malt, hop and special yeast. The name of the beer refers to the nickname of the Bruges townspeople, a name allegedly conferred upon them by Maximilian of Austria. In order to welcome the duke, the citizens paraded past him in a lavish procession of brightly coloured merrymakers and fools. When a short time later they asked their ruler to finance a new 'zothuis' or madhouse, his answer was as short as it was forceful: *'The only people I have seen here are fools. Bruges is one big madhouse. Just close the gates.'*

A splendid finish at Saint John's Hospital

Turn left into Zonnekemeers. Once across the water, enter the Oud Sint-Jan (Old St. John) site on the right.

The former St. John's Hospital (12th-19th century) **39**, which you can see in the right-hand corner, boasts a history stretching back more than 800 years. The oldest documents date from the year 1188! It was here that monks and nuns cared for pilgrims, travellers, the poor and the sick. Often, they came to the hospital to die. According to tradition, the painter Hans Memling was once a patient. After he was cured, he rewarded those who had treated him with four paintings. In the 19th century, two other Memling paintings found their way to the hospital, so that six of his masterpieces can now be admired here. Immediately in front of the convent of the old hospital stands the sculpture *The Veins of the Convent*, a work by the contemporary Italian artist Giuseppe Penone, which refers in a symbolic way to both the monastic way of life and the care function with which this site was once so closely associated.

Read more about Italian art in Bruges in the interview with Sonia Papili on pages 104-107.
Or how history still feeds the present – what could be more appropriate for a World Heritage City like Bruges!

Turn left at the corner and then go immediately right.
In the open space of the courtyard you will find the herb garden and the entrance to the 17th century pharmacy, which is well worth a visit. The herb garden contains all the necessary ingredients for 'gruut' or 'gruit', including lady's mantle, myrtle and laurel. You can find an explanation of what gruut is in *walk 2 on page 44*. Retrace your steps, turn left and walk through the passage. The entrance to the imposing medieval hospital wards, its church and chapel, the Diksmuide attic and the old dormitory are just around the corner to the right.

TIP

When you visit the Old St. John' Site, make sure you take a look at the 19th century infirmary wards. Some days, if you are lucky, you might catch a free concert by the Bruges harpist Luc Vanlaere. Moving and magical sounds that will make your visit to Bruges truly unforgettable. For more info, see www.harpmuziek.be

Walk 2
Bruges, a Burgundian city

When, during Bruges' Golden Age Philip the Bold, Duke of Burgundy, married Margaret of Dampierre, the daughter of the last Count of Flanders, the county of Flanders suddenly found itself belonging to Burgundy. As the Burgundian court liked to stay in Bruges, the port city became a magnet for noblemen, merchants and artists. They naturally all wanted to get their share of the city's wealth. Today the Burgundian influence is still strongly felt throughout Bruges. Let's discover a northern city with a southern character.

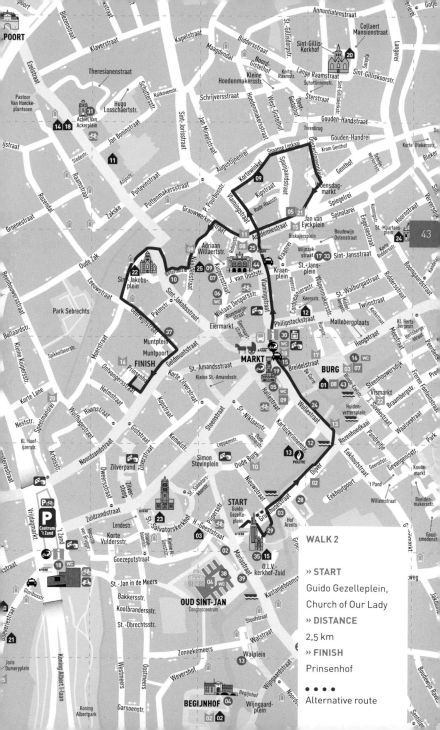

WALK 2

» START
Guido Gezelleplein,
Church of Our Lady

» DISTANCE
2,5 km

» FINISH
Prinsenhof

••••
Alternative route

From Guido Gezelleplein to Markt

This square is named after the Flemish priest and poet Guido Gezelle (1830-1899). Take a seat on one of the square's benches and enjoy Gezelle's lovely statue and the side-view of the Church of Our Lady **15** **35**. Its one hundred and fifteen (and a half!)-metre high brick tower is sure proof of the craftsmanship of Bruges' artisans. The church is currently undergoing largescale renovation work, so it is not possible to admire all its many fine works of art. However, Michelangelo's world-famous *Madonna and Child* can still be viewed. On your left is the striking residence of the lords of Gruuthuse, now the Gruuthuse Museum **29**. This, too, is undergoing renovation works and will be closed until 2018. The well (which unfortunately cannot be seen from the Guido Gezelleplein) and the tower were status symbols, and evidence of the Gruuthuse family's

great wealth. They made their fortune from their exclusive rights on 'gruut', a herb mixture that, ages before hop, was used to flavour beer. Louis of Gruuthuse not only commanded the army of Charles the Bold, he was also the personal bodyguard to Mary of Burgundy. In addition, he was a patron of the arts and the owner of the famous Gruuthuse manuscript that bears his name, a famous medieval collection of no fewer than 147 songs (amongst other things). His family motto 'Plus

est en vous' stands proudly above the door of the residence. Today, this translates as: 'There is more in you than you think'.

Continue along the narrow footpath to the left of the church. Due to renovation works, it is possible that this footpath will not be accessible.
Look up immediately beyond the bend. Do you see the chapel that seems to hold the Gruuthuse Museum and the Church of Our Lady in a close embrace? As the lords of Gruuthuse were far too grand to mingle with the populace, they had their own private chapel high above the street, where they could follow Mass.

Retrace your steps, cross the attractive Gruuthuseplein and turn right into Dijver.
Number 12 is the Groeninge Museum **28**, Bruges' most famous museum.
An interview with chief curator Till-Holger Borchert is on pages 112-115.
Further along Dijver is one of the locations of the College of Europe **02**, numbers 9-11, an international post-graduate institution that focuses on Europe.

Carry on down Dijver and turn left into Wollestraat.
Perez de Malvenda **13** is an impressive mansion on the corner of Wollestraat. This building, originally a mansion dating from the 13th century, has been restored from top to bottom and now houses a food store. Just before Markt are the Cloth Halls **09** , the Belfry's **05** warehouses and sales outlets. Facing the street, countless stalls were selling all sorts of herbs for medicinal purpose and potions. Indeed, Bruges being an important trading centre could by then import and sell a variety of herbs from all over Europe.

Markt, Bruges' beating heart

Wollestraat leads to Markt.
Markt is dominated by its Belfry **05**, for centuries the city's foremost edifice and the perfect lookout in case of war, fire or any other calamity. You can still climb to the top of the tower; but you

THE RIGHT TIME

On the Market Square (Markt), at the very top of the late-Gothic corner house 'Bouchoute', which is currently home to the Meridian 3 tearoom, there is a shining ball decorated with gold leaf. At the time of the inauguration of the Brussels-Ghent-Bruges railway line, people were aware that the clocks in Belgium did not all keep the same time. This problem was solved in Bruges in 1837 by Professor Quetelet, who 'drew' a meridian on the ground and set up a

Markt

noonday 'hand' that would show incontestably when it was twelve o'clock. This meridian ran diagonally over the Markt and is now marked by a series of copper nails. When the shadow of the golden ball falls on the meridian, it is midday precisely: 12.00 p.m. local solar time.

will need to conquer no fewer than 366 steps to get there! Fortunately, there are a couple of places during your ascent where you can stop for a breather. Once at the top you will be rewarded with an unforgettable panoramic view. At the foot of the Belfry are the world's most famous chippies ('frietkoten')! The statue of Jan Breydel and Pieter de Coninck graces the middle of the

TIP

As you are climbing your way to the top of the Belfry tower, why not stop for a break at the vaulted treasure chamber, where the city's charters, seal and public funds were all kept during medieval times. You can make a second stop at the 'Stenen Vloer' (Stone Floor): here you will learn everything you ever wanted to know about the clock, the drum and the carillon of 47 harmonious bells,

which together weigh a staggering 27 tons of pure bronze. With a little bit of luck you will be able to see the bell-ringer right at the very top, playing the keyboard with his fist, just a few steps below the bells themselves.

square. These two popular heroes of Bruges resisted French oppression and consequently played an important part during the Battle of the Golden Spurs in 1302. Their statue neatly looks out onto the Gothic revival style Provincial Court (Markt 3) 18 . Until the end of the 18th century, this side of the Markt was dominated by the Water Halls (Waterhalle), a large covered area where ships moored to be loaded and unloaded, right in the very heart of the city. In medieval times, the canals ran through and across the square, as indeed they still do, although they are now in underground tunnels. Do you feel like taking a relaxing break from all that walking? Then why not treat yourself to a coach ride and explore the city for an hour and a half from the luxury of a horse-drawn carriage *(see page 70)* or for 30 minutes from the back of a man-powered bike carriage *(see page 72)*. If neither of these is really your thing, you can always take the classic 50-minute City Tour by minibus *(see pages 70-71)*. Afterwards, you can simply resume your walk where you left off.

From Markt to Jan van Eyckplein

Keep Markt on your left and continue straight ahead to Vlamingstraat.
Since the 13th century, this used to be the harbour area's shopping street.
A fair number of banks had a branch here, and wine taverns were two a penny. Each of these had (and still has) a deep cellar where French and Rhenish wines

(see page 70)
(see page 72)
(see pages 70-71)

> **TIP**
>
> Since as long ago as 1897, two green painted mobile chippies have stood in front of the Belfry. It is definitely the best place in town to buy – and sell – chips, good for the annual consumption of several tons of fast food! The stalls are open nearly every hour of the day and night, so that you never need to go hungry!

could easily be stacked. In the medieval vaulted cellars of Taverne Curiosa (Vlamingstraat 22), the alcohol-laden atmosphere of those bygone days can still be inhaled. Halfway along Vlamingstraat is the elegant City Theatre 44 on your left. This royal theatre (1869) is one of Europe's best-preserved city theatres. Behind the Neo-Renaissance façade lie a magnificent auditorium and a palatial foyer. Papageno, the bird seller from

Vlamingstraat

SWANS ON THE CANALS

After the death of Mary of Burgundy (1482), Bruges went through some troubled times. The townspeople, enraged by new taxes Maximilian of Austria, Mary's successor, had imposed upon them, rose in revolt against their new ruler. As Maximilian was locked up in House Craenenburg on the Market Square, he helplessly witnessed the torture and eventual beheading of his bailiff and trusted councillor Pieter Lanchals (Long Neck). A rusty old legend says that when the duke came back to power, he took his vengeance on the local people by forcing them to keep 'long necks' or swans on the canals for all time. In reality, however, swans have been swimming on the canals since the beginning of the 15ᵗʰ century, when they were seen as a status symbol of the city's power and wealth.

Mozart's opera, *The Magic Flute*, guards the entrance. His score lies scattered on the square opposite.

Continue along Vlamingstraat and turn right into Kortewinkel just before the water.

Somewhat hidden from gazing eyes, Kortewinkel boasts a unique 16ᵗʰ-century wooden house front. It is one of only two left in the city (you will come across the other one further along this walk). Just a few metres on is another exciting discovery at number 10. The former Jesuit House 09 has a magnificent hidden courtyard garden. Is its door open? Then walk in and enjoy its heavenly peace.

Kortewinkel turns into Spaanse Loskaai, the home port of the Spanish merchants until the end of the 16ᵗʰ century.

The picturesque bridge on your left is the Augustine Bridge, one of Bruges' oldest specimens, with its seven hundred summers. The stone seats were originally intended to display the wares of the diligent sellers. The bridge affords an excellent view of the house in the right-hand corner, which connects Spanjaardstraat with Kortewinkel. This was once House De Noodt Gods but is also said to be a haunted house, according to the locals. When an amorous monk was rejected by a nun, the man murdered her and then committed suicide. Ever since they have been haunting that ramshackle building...

Continue along Spaanse Loskaai, go down the first street on your right and proceed to Oosterlingenplein.
During Bruges' Golden Age this was the fixed abode of the so-called 'Oosterlingen' (Easteners) or German merchants. Their imposing warehouse took up the entire left corner of the square. Today the only remnant is the building to the right of Hotel Bryghia. Their warehouse must have been truly grand!

Genthof

Beyond Oosterlingenplein is Woensdagmarkt, the square on which the statue of the painter Hans Memling attracts all attention. Turn right into Genthof.
Here the second of two authentic medieval wooden house fronts draws attention. Notice that each floor juts out a little more than the next one. This building technique, which helped to avoid water damage (but also created extra space), was consequently used in various architectural styles.

Burgundian Manhattan

Proceed to Jan van Eyckplein.
This was the Manhattan of Burgundian Bruges, the place where everything happened. It was here that ships moored, were loaded and unload, and paid their tolls. In this unremitting hustle and bustle a cacophony of languages was heard above the din, one sounding even louder than the other. What a soundtrack! Each business transaction required a few local sounds too, of course, as there always had to be a Bruges broker present who

TIP

The Genthof has in recent years attracted a variety of different arts and crafts. There is a glass-blower, a trendy vintage store and a number of contemporary art galleries. And on the corner you can find 't Terrastje, the café with probably the smallest terrace in Bruges.

05 15 21

would naturally pocket his cut. On the corner, the 16th-century House De Rode Steen (number 8) has been sparkling in all its glory since its restoration (the first building in Bruges to be renovated thanks to a subsidy from the city) in 1877. At numbers 1-2 is the Old Tollhouse (1477) **05** **21**, where the tolls levied on the goods and products of both regional and international trade were collected. On the left-hand side of this truly monumental building stands the Rijkepijnders House, the smallest house in Bruges. This was the meeting place of the *rijkepijnders*, the agents who supervised the porters and the dockworkers employed to load and unload the ships. People with sharp eyes may be able to spot some of these heavily-laden *pijnders* depicted on the facade.

Continue along Academiestraat.
Right on the corner with Jan van Eyck-

plein is another remarkable building, distinguished by its striking tower. This is the Burghers' Lodge (Poortersloge) **15**, a 15th-century building where the burgesses of the city (patricians and merchants) once used to meet. In a wall niche, the Bruges Bear, an important city symbol, stands proud and upright. From 1720 to 1890, the Burghers' Lodge housed the Municipal Academy of Fine Arts. From 1912 to 2012, the building served as the home of the State Archives.

Proceed to Grauwwerkersstraat.
The little square connecting Academiestraat with Grauwwerkersstraat has been known as 'Beursplein' since time immemorial.
Here merchants were engaged in high-quality trade. The merchant houses of Genoa (Genuese Lodge, later renamed 'Saaihalle' **08**, and today Belgian Fries

THE LITTLE BEAR OF BRUGES

When Baldwin Iron Arm, the first Count of Flanders, visited Bruges for the first time, the first creature he saw was a big 'white' bear. According to the legend, all this happened in the 9th century. After a fierce fight the count succeeded in killing the animal. In homage to the courageous beast, he proclaimed the bear to be the city's very own symbol. Today 'Bruges' oldest inhabitant' in the niche of the Burghers' Lodge is festively rigged out during exceptional celebrations. The Bruges Bear is holding the coat of arms of the Noble Company of the White Bear, a chivalric order of knights famed for their jousting tournaments, which was founded shortly after Baldwin I had beaten the 'white' bear and which held its meetings in the Burghers' Lodge.

Museum (Frietmuseum) **25**), Florence (now De Florentijnen restaurant) and Venice (now poolbar The Monk) once stood here side by side like brothers. In front of house Ter Beurse (1276) **11**, the central inn, merchants from all over Europe used to gather to arrange business appointments and conduct exchange transactions. The Dutch word for stock exchange became 'beurs', derived from the name of the house. Many other languages would take over this term, such as French (bourse) or Italian (borsa).

Turn into Grauwwerkersstraat and stop immediately in your tracks. The side wall of house Ter Beurse **11**, and more precisely the part between the two sets of ground-floor windows, bears the signatures of the stonecutters. This way everybody knew which mason cut which stones and how much each mason had to be paid. The house next-door to house Ter Beurse, called 'de Kleine Beurse' (the Little Stock Exchange), still sits on its original street level.

PRINSENHOF GOSSIP

> As Philip the Good hadn't yet laid eyes on his future wife (Isabella of Portugal), he sent Jan van Eyck to Portugal to paint her portrait. This way the duke wanted to make certain he had made the right choice. The duke's ploy worked, because history teaches us that the couple had a happy marriage.

> Although the popular Mary of Burgundy incurred only seemingly minor injuries as a result of a fall with her horse, the accident would eventually lead to her death from a punctured lung at Prinsenhof. Back in those times there was no cure for inflammation.

> During the hotel renovation no fewer than 578 silver coins, minted between 1755 and 1787, were dug up. After some careful counting and calculations it is assumed that the energetic English nuns, who lived there at that time, entrusted the coins to the soil so as to prevent the advancing French troops from stealing their hard-earned capital.

Turn left into Naaldenstraat.
On your right, Bladelin Court **09** with its attractive tower looms up ahead. In the 15th-16th century, Pieter Bladelin, portrayed above the gate whilst praying to the Virgin Mary, leased his house to the Florentine banking family of de' Medici, who set up one of their branches here. Today, this property is owned by the Catholic University of Leuven and the Sisters of Our Lady of the Seven Sorrows.

Somewhat further along, next to another ornamental tower, turn right into Boterhuis, a winding cobbled alley that catapults you back straight into the Middle Ages. Keep right, pass Saint James's Church and turn left into Moerstraat.
The Dukes of Burgundy and the vast majority of foreign merchants patronised Saint James's Church **22**. Their extrav-

agant gifts have left their glittering mark on the interior.

Prinsenhof (the Princes' Court), home base of the Dukes of Burgundy

Turn left into Geerwijnstraat and carry on to Muntplein.
Muntplein (Coin Square) belonged to nearby Prinsenhof **16**. As you might have guessed, this was where Bruges' mint was situated. The statue *Flandria*

TIP

Behind the street Boterhuis, at Sint-Jakobsstraat 26, you will find Cinema Lumière **10**, purveyor of the better kind of artistic film. In other words, the place to be for real film-lovers.

Nostra (Our Flanders), which represents a noblewoman on horseback, was designed by the Belgian sculptor Jules Lagae (1862-1931).

At the end of Geerwijnstraat turn right into Geldmuntstraat. The walk's finishing point is Prinsenhof.

We end the walk on a highlight. Prinsenhof used to be the palace of the Flemish counts and Burgundy dukes. This impressive mansion, originally seven times the size of what you see today, was expanded in the 15th century by Philip the Good to celebrate his (third) marriage to Isabella of Portugal. When Charles the Bold remarried Margaret of York, the largest bathhouse in Europe, a game court (to play 'jeu de paume' or the palm game, the forerunner of tennis) and a zoological garden were all added to the ducal residence. It is no surprise that Prinsenhof not only became the favourite pied-à-terre of the Dukes of Burgundy, but also the nerve centre of their political, economic and cultural ambitions. Both Philip the Good (d.1467) and Mary of Burgundy (d.1482) breathed their last here. After the death of the popular Mary of Burgundy the palace's fortunes declined, until it eventually ended up in private hands. In the 17th century, English nuns converted it into a boarding school for girls of well-to-do parents. Nowadays you can stay in the Prinsenhof Castle in true princely style.

> TIP
>
> Whoever wants to get a really good impression of the magnificence of this city castle and its elegant gardens should follow the signs in the Ontvangersstraat to the hotel car park at Moerstraat 46. Of course, you can always treat yourself – and your nearest and dearest – to a princely drink in the bar of the hotel: the perfect way to enjoy the grandeur and luxury of the complex.

Walk 3
Strolling through silent Bruges

Although the parishes of Saint Anne and Saint Giles are known as places of great tranquillity, the fact that they are off the beaten track does
not mean that the visitor will be short of adventure. How about a row of
nostalgic windmills? Or perhaps some unpretentious working-class
neighbourhoods or a couple of exclusive gentlemen's clubs? Will you
be able to absorb all these impressions serenely? Don't worry. After
the tour we invite you to catch your breath in Bruges' oldest cafe!

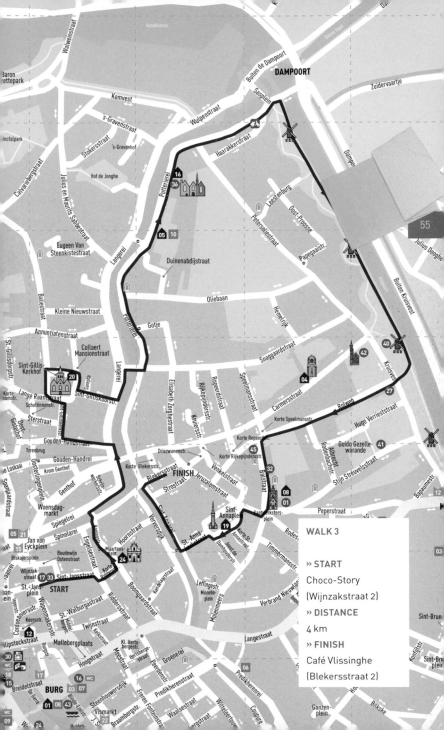

DAMPOORT

55

WALK 3

» START
Choco-Story
(Wijnzakstraat 2)

» DISTANCE
4 km

» FINISH
Café Vlissinghe
(Blekersstraat 2)

From Choco-Story to Gouden-Handstraat

Choco-Story (Chocolate Museum) **17** is the perfect starting point for the longest walk in this guide. This museum not only dips you in the yummy history of chocolate and cocoa, it also offers extensive chocolate tasting. If you wish, you can also buy your supplies here. No doubt the chocolate will help you to keep up a brisk pace! At the same address Lumina Domestica **33** contains the world's largest collection of lamps and lights. The museum also houses 6,000 antiques.

Turn left into Sint-Jansstraat, carry on to Korte Riddersstraat and continue until the end of the street. Saint Walburga's Church **24** rises up in all its magnificence right in front of you. This Baroque edifice (1619-1642) boasts a remarkable marble communion rail and high altar. Nearby, at number 3 there is a splendid 18th-century mansion.

Continue down Koningstraat to the bridge.
This bridge, which connects poetic Spinolarei with Spiegelrei, affords a lovely view of Oud Huis Amsterdam on your left. Today this historic town house (Spiegelrei 3) is an elegant hotel. This part of the city used to be mainly populated by the English and Scots. The English merchants even had their own 'steegere' or stair where their goods were unloaded. The stair is still there, and the street connecting it is appropriately called Engelse-straat. The dignified white school building (number 15) across the bridge was once a college of English Jesuits.

Saint Giles', home base of workmen and artists

Cross the bridge, turn right along Spiegelrei and turn into Gouden-Handstraat, the fourth street on your left.
In the 15th century Gouden-Handstraat and the parish of Saint Giles were known as the artists' quarter. Hans Memling may have lived a few streets further down in Sint-Jorisstraat; the fact of the matter is that Jan van Eyck had a studio in Gouden-Handstraat, and that his somewhat lesser known fellow artists also used to congregate in this neighbourhood.

Turn right into Sint-Gilliskerkstraat. This street bumps into Saint Giles's Church  20 in the heart of the tranquil quarter of Saint Giles'. Initially a chapel, this building was upgraded to a parish church in 1258. In spite of its interior in Gothic revival style and its superb paintings, the church takes on the appearance of a simple, sturdy village church. Don't be misled. In and around the church countless famous painters were buried, such as Hans Memling (d.1494), in his time the best-paid painter, Lanceloot Blondeel (d.1561) and Pieter Pourbus (d.1584). Their graves and the cemetery may have disappeared, but their artists' souls still hover in the air.

Walk around the church and turn into Sint-Gilliskoorstraat.
Although the workmen's dwellings in these streets are rather small, they nevertheless display a bricked up window. As it happened, a tax on windows was levied in 1800. As a consequence, a large number of windows were walled up.

From Potterierei to the vesten (ramparts)

Turn left into Langerei at the end of the street. Cross the lovely Snaggaardbrug, the first bridge you get to, into Potterierei. Turn left and follow the canal for some time.

After a fair distance along Potterierei is Bruges' Major Seminary (number 72) 05 on your right. A unique place with a lush orchard and meadows with cows at pasture. Between 1628 and 1642 a new Cistercian Abbey (the Dune Abbey) was erected here, which later

Woensdagmarkt

BRUGES AND THE SEA

For centuries, Potterierei ensured the city's wealth. This canal ran to Damme where it was connected to a large lock, called 'Speie', which in turn was connected to the Zwin, a deep sea channel and tidal inlet. While Damme developed into an outport, Bruges grew into Northwestern Europe's greatest business centre of the Middle Ages. The arts flourished, culture thrived, prosperity seemed to be set for all eternity. The tide turned when Mary of Burgundy suddenly passed away in 1482. The relations between Bruges and the Burgundians turned sour and the Burgundian court left the city. The foreign merchants and their wealth followed in its wake. The Zwin continued to silt up and Bruges lost her privileged commercial position. As a result, and compounded by a series of political intrigues, the city fell into a deep winter sleep.

on would achieve great fame for the wealth and erudition of its occupants. During the French Revolution, the abbey was brought under public ownership, and the abbot and monks were chased away. The 17th-century abbey buildings were first used as a military hospital and then as a military depot and a grammar school before they were eventually taken over by the Major Seminary in 1833. Up to the present day the Seminary has been training Catholic priests here. Nowadays, there is also a research and training centre for the University of the United Nations 10. Just a few yards further down at number 79B is Our Lady of the Pottery 16 36. Its history goes back to the 13th century. Diligent nuns used to treat pilgrims, travellers and the sick here. From the 15th century onwards, it also became a home for the care of the elderly. The Gothic church with its Baroque interior and its rich collection of works of art, accumulated by the

hospital throughout the centuries, is a hidden gem that is certainly well worth a visit!

Carry on to the lock and spend some time by the water.
This idyllic spot is where the canal

05 10

Damse Vaart heads out across the other side of the ring road towards the equally romantic town of Damme. It's hard to believe that this area around the canal was once a scene of great controversy. Up until the Eighty Years' War, Bruges was connected to Sluis by way of Damme. Ambitious Napoleon Bonaparte had the link with the tidal inlet of the Zwin, the natural predecessor of the Damse Vaart, dredged by Spanish prisoners of war so as to create a watercourse that would run all the way to Antwerp. His plan then was to develop the port city of Antwerp into a naval base, which would enable him to avoid the English sea blockade. Napoleon's project left Damme cut in twain. The wild plans of the little general were never carried out in full, and by 1814 Napoleon's role in Flanders had come to an end. Under the impulse of William I, King of the Netherlands, who also saw the value of a connecting canal, the digging work continued until 1824. Belgian independence (1830) meant that the project was finally terminated, by which time it had reached as far as Sluis. Today the low-traffic bicycle path skirting the canal is a most attractive route linking Bruges with Damme. The trip is highly recommended, as it traverses *le plat pays*, that flat country made famous by Jacques Brel in the moving song of that name. Imagine! In the middle of a unique polder landscape this truly poetic canal strip, bordered by lofty poplars bended down by eternal westerly winds.

TIP

Have we made you curious? Or do you just like to do things the easy way? If so, leave your bike and car at home and 'all aboard' for a voyage on the Lamme Goedzak 🚋 , the most stylish way to reach the town of Damme. Step back in time during this nostalgic journey. *(For more information see page 67)*

Sasplein

THE ARCHERS' GUILD: 120 MEN AND 2 QUEENS!

Two centuries-old archery clubs are now to be found in what for many years was one of the poorer districts of Bruges. High and dry on the same hill as the Sint-Janshuis Mill, at the bottom left, stands the Sint-Joris (St. George's) Guild **41**, a crossbow guild that specializes in two archery disciplines: shooting at targets on the ground and shooting at feathered discs in a tower. To the right, with its eye-catching target tower, is the home of the Sint-Sebastiaan (St. Sebastian) Guild **42**, a long-bow society. This guild goes back more than six centuries, which makes it unique in the world. The society numbers 120 male members exactly and two notable female honorary members: the Belgian queen Mathilde and the British queen. Ever since the exiled English king Charles II took up residence in Bruges in the 17th century, the city and the British Royal Family have always been closely associated. Within the St. Sebastian Archery Guild, Charles founded both the British Grenadier Guards and the Life Guards Regiment.

Turn right and carry on along the Vesten (ramparts), which surround the city like a ring of green.

In the 16th century, more than thirty windmills were turning their sails here. Today only four are left. In the 18th century, the millers stood by helplessly when bread consumption took a dive and people started to consume more potatoes. Eventually steam machines would take over the millers' tasks. One of the mills, the Sint-Janshuis Mill **40** can still be visited today. A miller will be happy not only to give you an explanation of his craft, but also show you how the milling is done. It is well worth climbing the slopes on which the Sint-Janshuis Mill and the Bonne Chiere Mill (near the Kruispoort/Cross Gate **12**) proudly stand. The hills afford a fantastic panoramic view of the city. This is the perfect spot to brush up on your amassed knowledge of Bruges. And there's more! Down below on your right is the Verloren Hoek (the Lost Corner), now an authentic working-class district, but back in the 19th century an impoverished neighbourhood with such a bad reputation that even the police didn't dare enter its streets.

40

Silent Bruges

Descend down the slope and turn right into Rolweg.

Right on the corner is the Gezelle Museum **27**, the birthplace of Guido Gezelle (1830-1899), one of Flanders' most venerable poets. On display are handwritten letters, writing material and a deliciously peaceful garden with an age-old Corsican pine. Gezelle's parents worked here as gardener and

caretaker, in exchange for which they and their family received free board and lodging. Little Guido grew up in these idyllic surroundings. He would eventually return to Bruges many years later and after many a peregrination. Upon his return he became curate of Saint Walburga's Church **24**. He also took over the running of the English Convent **04**, where he would die. These were his last words, reportedly: *'I have so loved hearing the birds singing.'* Here, in this most verdant part of Bruges, we still know precisely what the priest and poet meant.

Turn into Balstraat, the second street on the left.

This picturesque working-man's alley houses the Museum of Folk Life (Volkskundemuseum) **45**. The 17th-century row of single-room dwellings, restored and converted into authentic artisans' interiors such as a milliner's, a confectioner's and a small classroom, will

TIP

Interested in a little something 'extra'? Then go and take a look at the Albrecht Rodenbachstraat, another of the city's hidden gems. This green suburb avant la lettre offers an almost unbroken succession of stepgables and other fascinating facades, each fronted by a delightful little garden.

take you back to bygone days. The tower of the 15th-century Jerusalem Chapel **08** can easily be spotted from these premises. This chapel was commissioned by the Adornes, a prominent Bruges merchant family of Genovese origin, who lived in a magnificent mansion **01** on the Peperstraat. In 1470, Anselm Adornes collected one of his sons (the father had no fewer than sixteen children) in Padua to set off on a pilgrimage to the Holy Land. Upon his return to Bruges, Anselm decided to build an exact copy of the Church of the Holy Sepulchre. The result was remarkable.

In the adjacent Adornes Estate **01**, you will make closer acquaintance with this prominent family and its intriguing history.

TIP

If you feel like taking a break, you are welcome to rest your tired feet in the large, walled garden of the Museum of Folk Life. It is a delightful oasis of calm in the heart of the city, and even has its own outdoor pétanque alley! At Balstraat 16, you can visit the Lace Centre **32**, which has been installed in the fully renovated old lace School. If you visit during one of the many lace demonstrations (2.00-5.00 p.m., not on Sunday and public holidays), it is almost like stepping back in time.

At the crossroads turn right into Jeruzalemstraat; then, at the church, left unto Sint-Annaplein.

The tiny square is dominated by the ap-

parently simple Church of Saint Anne **19**. Its exterior may be austere, but its interior is one of Bruges' most splendid examples of Baroque architecture. As this neighbourhood gradually became more prestigious, the church did the same!

With the church behind you, follow the Sint-Annakerkstraat and then turn right into Sint-Annarei.
At the corner of the confluence of the two waterways one of Bruges' most handsome town houses is proudly showing off its Rococo credentials (Sint-Annarei no. 22). Sit yourself down

on a shady bench and enjoy this exceptional prospect.

Retrace your steps for just a few yards and turn left into Blekersstraat next to the bridge.
Café Vlissinghe at number 2 is undoubtedly Bruges' oldest café. This has been a tavern since 1515. It is no surprise then that you will find oodles of ambiance here. It is therefore the perfect place to settle down and let the wonderful memories of your walk slowly sink in. A local beer will be your ideal companion. Cheers!

Café Vlissinghe

Rozenhoedkaai

Know your way around
Bruges

Exploring Bruges

You might want to stroll, amble and saunter down the streets of Bruges all day long. However, why not try to see the city from a different perspective? During a walking or bicycle tour, a guide will show you numerous secret places. Maybe you would prefer a boat trip on the mysterious canals – an unforgettable experience! And a ride in a horse-drawn carriage must surely be the perfect romantic outing. Sport-lovers can even do a guided run around the city. Or perhaps you simply want to tour all the highlights as quickly and as comfortably as possible? Then a minibus with expert commentary is what you need. Or what about a flight in a hot-air balloon or a tour in a bike carriage? The choice is yours!

🚤 Bruges by boat

A visit to Bruges isn't complete without a boat trip on its canals. Jump aboard at any of the five landing stages (consult city map) for a half-hour trip that allows you to appreciate the most noteworthy delights of the city from a completely different angle.

OPEN > Sailings are guaranteed from March to mid-November: in principle, daily from 10.00 a.m. to 6.00 p.m., last departure at 5.30 p.m.

PRICE > € 8.00; children aged 4 to 11 (accompanied by an adult): € 4.00; children under 4: free

🚂 Lamme Goedzak (steam wheeler) Damme

The nostalgic river boat 'Lamme Goedzak', with room for 170 passengers, sails back and forth between Bruges and the centre of Damme, the town of the local folk hero Tijl Uilenspiegel (Owlglass), whose friend was called ... Lamme Goedzak!

OPEN > During the period 1/4 to 30/9: departures from Bruges to Damme, daily at 10.00 a.m., 12.00 p.m., 2.00 p.m. and 4.00 p.m.; departures from Damme to Bruges, daily at 11.00 a.m., 1.00 p.m., 3.00 p.m. and 5.00 p.m.

PRICE > € 8.00 (one-way ticket) or € 11.00 (return ticket); 65+: € 7.50 (one-way ticket) or € 10.00 (return ticket); children aged 3 to 11: € 6.50 (one-way ticket) or € 9.00 (return ticket)

MEETING POINT > Embark in Bruges at the Noorweegse Kaai 31 (City map: J1)

INFO > Tel. +32 (0)50 28 86 10, www.bootdamme-brugge.be; public transport: scheduled bus no. 4, bus stop: Sasplein near the Dampoort; from there it is a 5-10 minute walk to the landing stage in Bruges.

Port Cruise Zeebrugge

The port cruise departs from the old fishing port on board of the Zephira, a passenger ship. The tour takes in the naval base, the Pierre Vandamme Lock

(one of the largest locks in the world), the gas terminal, the wind turbine park, the 'tern' island, the cruise ships and the dredging vessels. You will also see how the massive container ships are unloaded at the quay. Each visitor is given an easy-to-use audio-visual guide in the desired language. An experience that offers a unique insight into the port and its manifold activities.

OPEN > During the period 1/4 to 15/10: weekends and public holidays at 2.00 p.m.; during the period 1/7 to 31/8: daily at 2.00 p.m. and 4.00 p.m; during the period 1/8 to 15/8: daily extra round trip at 11.00 a.m.

PRICE > € 9.50; 60+ and students: € 9.00; children aged 3 to 11: € 7.00. Tickets are purchased on board

MEETING POINT > Embark at the landing stage at the end of the Tijdokstraat (old fishing port), Zeebrugge

LANGUAGES > English, Dutch, French, German. You can also download the commentary on your smartphone.

INFO > Tel. +32 (0)59 70 62 94 (for extra departures outside the fixed sailing times), www.franlis.be; public transport: train Bruges-Zeebrugge, from the station Zeebrugge-Dorp: about 15 to 20 minutes on foot or from the station Zeebrugge-Strand: coast tram (direction: Knokke), to tram stop: Zeebrugge-Kerk (church) and then a 5 minute walk

Bruges by heart

A quality walk with local guides

Would you like to explore Bruges with someone who really knows the city? If so, hurry on down to one of the ℹ️ information offices on 't Zand (Concertgebouw) or the Markt (Historium). Here you can register to take part in a wonderful walk full of history old and new, fascinating facts and figures, fun stories and insider tips. There is no-one better able to show you the beauty of the city in all its many facets than an official guide.

OPEN > You can see when walks can be reserved on www.visitbruges.be. Or else you can just call in at one of the ℹ️ information offices.

PRICE > € 12.50; children under 12: free

MEETING POINT > The walk starts at the ℹ️ tourist office 't Zand (Concertgebouw)

LANGUAGES > English, Dutch, French, Spanish

TICKETS > ℹ️ Tourist office at the Markt (Historium), 't Zand (Concertgebouw) and www.ticketsbrugge.be

APP > A different way to explore Bruges on foot (or by bike) is by using the free Xplore Bruges-app.

More information can be found on www.xplorebruges.be or on page 106.

INFO > Tel. +32 (0)50 44 46 46, www.visitbruges.be

Photo Tour Brugge

Whether you are a photography expert or a photography novice, during the Photo Tour Andy McSweeney takes you to all the most photogenic spots in the city! What are the 'must have' shots for the photo reportage of your city trip to Bruges? You will find out during a fascinating exploration of the city, complete with dozens of practical photography tips from Andy.

(Read more about Andy McSweeney in the interview on page 136-139.)

OPEN > Four walks are organized each day, each with a different theme: 'Edges of Brugge' (10.00 a.m.-12.00 p.m.) focuses on the side streets and canals; 'Essential Brugge' (1.00 p.m.-3.00 p.m.) zooms in on the top sights; during 'Hidden Brugge' (4.00 p.m.-6.00 p.m.) you will go in search of some of the city's less well known corners; the private tour 'Shades of Brugge' (8.00 p.m.-11.00 p.m.) allows you to experience the evening delights of the city.

PRICE > € 50.00; private tour: € 200.00; every paying participant will receive 5 photos of Bruges taken by Andy McSweeney; each photographing participant can bring along a non-photographing partner free of charge; max. of 5 photographers per tour, with the exception of the private tour (max. 3 photographers). Prior reservation is necessary, but is possible on the day itself.

MEETING POINT > Basilica of the Holy Blood, on the Burg square

LANGUAGES > English, but also Dutch and/or French on request

INFO > Tel. +32 (0)486 17 52 75, www.phototourbrugge.com

Running around Bruges

Tourist Run Brugge – guided tours
Accompanied by a guide you run – at a gentle pace – through the streets and alleyways of Bruges. Because you either

run early in the morning or early in the evening, you can freely admire Bruges. The circuit, which ends on the Markt, is 9.5 km long. With the explanation that you receive along the way, you should allow 1 to 1.5 hours for completion.

OPEN > Daily, 7.00 a.m., 8.00 a.m., 9.00 a.m., 5.00 p.m., 6.00 p.m., 7.00 p.m., 8.00 p.m. and 9.00 p.m. Reservation is required.

PRICE > € 30.00/person; for 2 runners: € 25.00/person; 3 runners or more: € 20.00/person

MEETING POINT > At the statue of Jan Breydel and Pieter de Coninck on the Markt. If requested in advance, you can be picked up from wherever you are staying (hotel, etc.).

LANGUAGES > English, Dutch, French, German

INFO > Tel. +32 (0)473 88 37 17, www.touristrunbrugge.be

Bruges by horse-drawn carriage

The carriage ride along Bruges' historic winding streets takes thirty minutes. About half way through the tour, the horse and carriage makes a short stop at the Beguinage. Throughout the journey, the driver will give an expert commentary.

OPEN > Daily, 9.00 a.m. to at least 6.00 p.m., but no later than 10.00 p.m.

PRICE PER CARRIAGE > € 50.00; max. 5 persons

MEETING POINT > Markt, but at the Burg square on Wednesday morning (market day)

INFO > www.hippo.be/koets

Bruges by bus

City Tour Bruges

The mini buses of City Tour provide a guided tour that will take you past all the most beautiful places in Bruges. Every half hour, they depart for a 50 minutes drive along the most important highlights of the town.

OPEN > Daily, every half hour (also on Sundays and public holidays). The first bus leaves at 10.00 a.m. During the periods 1/1 to 31/1 and 1/11 to 31/12 the last bus

leaves at 4.00 p.m.; during the period 1/2 to 9/2 at 4.30 p.m.; during the period 10/2 to 28/2 at 5.00 p.m.; during the periods 1/3 to 15/3 and 16/10 to 31/10 at 5.30 p.m.; during the periods 16/3 to 30/4 and 1/10 to 15/10 at 6.00 p.m. and during the period 1/5 to 30/9 at 7.00 p.m. There are no departures at 1.30 p.m. and 6.30 p.m.

PRICE > € 20.00; children aged 6 to 11 years: € 15.00; children under 6: free

MEETING POINT > Markt

LANGUAGES > Individual headphones provide a private commentary (16 languages available)

INFO > Tel. +32 (0)50 35 50 24 (Monday to Friday, 10.00 a.m.-12.00 p.m.), www.citytour.be

Bruges by bike

QuasiMundo Biketours:
Bruges by bike

Riding through the narrow streets, you will discover the charming character of medieval Bruges. The fascinating stories of the guide will catapult you back in time to the era when counts and dukes ruled over the city. On the way, of course, you will stop to enjoy a thirst-quenching Belgian beer.

OPEN > During the period 15/3 to 23/12: daily, 10.00 a.m.-12.30 p.m. Reservation is required.

PRICE > Including bike, guide, raincoat and drink in a local bar: € 30.00; youngsters aged 9 to 26 and students: € 28.00. If you bring your own bike, then the rates are as follows: adults: € 18.00; youngsters (aged 9 to 26) and students: € 16.00. Children under 9: free

MEETING POINT > At the City Hall on the Burg square, 10 minutes before departure

LANGUAGES > English, other languages on request

INFO > Tel. +32 (0)50 33 07 75 or +32 (0)478 28 15 21, www.quasimundo.eu

(See also 'Guided excursions from Bruges', page 156.)

NEW Bruges by bike carriage

Fietskoetsen Brugge

Discover all the city's most romantic places and historical sites of interest in a unique and ecological way. A personal guide will take you on a bike carriage tour of 30 minutes.

OPEN > During the period 1/4 to 31/1: daily, 10.00 a.m.-8.00 p.m.; during the period 1/2 to 31/3: on Saturday and Sunday, 10.00 a.m.-8.00 p.m.

PRICE PER BIKE CARRIAGE > € 24.00; max. 3 persons

MEETING POINT > On the Markt, outside the De Reyghere book store; but on the Burg square on Wednesday mornings

LANGUAGES > English, Dutch, French, German and Spanish

INFO > Tel. +32 (0)478 40 95 57, www.fietskoetsenbrugge.be

Bruges by hot air balloon

Bruges Ballooning

The most adventurous and probably the most romantic way to discover Bruges is by hot-air balloon. Bruges Ballooning organizes both a morning flight (including a champagne breakfast) and an evening flight (including a bite to eat, champagne or a beer) over Bruges. The whole trip lasts for three hours, with at least one hour in the air.

OPEN > During the period 1/4 to 12/11: daily flights, but only if booked in advance; bookings can be made on the day itself with a few hours' notice, providing there are no prior reservations.

PRICE > € 180.00; children aged 4 to 12: € 110.00

MEETING POINT > You will be picked up and dropped off wherever you are staying.

LANGUAGES > English, Dutch, French and Spanish

INFO > Tel. +32 (0)475 97 28 87, www.bruges-ballooning.com

Museums, places of interest and attractions

Some places are so special, so breathtaking or so unique that you simply have to see them. Bruges is filled to the brim with wonderful witnesses of a prosperous past. Although the Flemish primitives are undoubtedly Bruges' showpiece attraction, museum devotees in search of much more will not be disappointed. Indeed, the Bruges range of attractions is truly magnificent. From modern plastic art by way of Michelangelo's world-famous *Madonna and Child* to the brand new Lace Centre. It's all there for you to discover!

01 08 Adornesdomein – Jeruzalemkapel (Adornes Estate – Jerusalem Chapel)

The Adornes domain consists of the 15th-century Jerusalem Chapel (a jewel of medieval architecture built by this rich merchant family), the Adornes mansion and a series of adjacent alms-houses. In the multimedia museum, you can follow in the footsteps of Anselm Adornes and learn all about the world in which he lived. You will go on a pilgrim-age, take part in a joust and meet many notable persons of the time, such as the King of Scotland, the Lords of Gruuthuse and the Dukes of Burgundy.

OPEN > Monday to Saturday, 10.00 a.m.-5.00 p.m.

ADDITIONAL CLOSING DATES >
All (Belgian) public holidays
PRICE > € 7.00; 65+: € 5.00; youngsters aged 7 to 25: € 3.50; children under 7: free
INFO > Peperstraat 3A, tel. +32 (0)50 33 88 83, www.adornes.org

02 Archeologiemuseum (Archaeological Museum)

This museum presents the unwritten history of Bruges. Its motto: feel your past beneath your feet. Discover the history of the city through different kinds of search and hands-on activities. A fascinating mix of archaeological finds, riddles, replicas and reconstruc-tions shed light on daily life in times gone by, from the home to the work-place and from birth till death.

OPEN > Tuesday to Sunday, 9.30 a.m.-12.30 p.m. and 1.30 p.m.-5.00 p.m., last admission: 12.00 p.m. and 4.30 p.m. (open on Easter Monday and Whit Monday)

ADDITIONAL CLOSING DATES >
1/1, 25/5 (1.00 p.m.-5.00 p.m.) and 25/12
PRICE > € 4.00; 65+ and youngsters aged 12 to 25: € 3.00; children under 12: free
INFO > Mariastraat 36A, tel. +32 (0)50 44 87 43, www.museabrugge.be

03 Arentshuis

In this elegant 17th-century mansion with its picturesque garden, the work of the versatile British artist Frank Brangwyn (1867-1956) is on display on the top floor. Brangwyn was both a graphic artist and a painter, as well as a designer of car-pets, furniture and ceramics. The ground floor is the setting for temporary plastic art exhibitions.

OPEN > Tuesday to Sunday, 9.30 a.m.-
5.00 p.m., last admission: 4.30 p.m. (open
on Easter Monday and Whit Monday)
ADDITIONAL CLOSING DATES >
1/1, 25/5 (1.00 p.m.-5.00 p.m.) and 25/12
PRICE > € 4.00; 65+ and youngsters
aged 12 to 25: € 3.00; children under 12:
free; combination ticket with Groeninge
Museum possible *(see page 84)*
INFO > Dijver 16, tel. +32 (0)50 44 87 43,
www.museabrugge.be

🦽 **01** Basiliek van het Heilig Bloed (Basilica of the Holy Blood)

The double church, dedicated to Our
Lady and Saint Basil in the 12th century
and a basilica since 1923, consists of a
lower church that has maintained its
Romanesque character and a
neo-Gothic upper church, in which the
relic of the Holy Blood is preserved.
The treasury, with numerous valuable
works of art, is also worth a visit.
OPEN > Daily, 9.30 a.m.-12.00 p.m. and
2.00 p.m.-5.00 p.m.; during the period
16/11 to 31/3 closed on Wednesday afternoon. Veneration of the relic: daily, 11.30
a.m.-12.00 p.m. and 2.00 p.m.-4.00 p.m.

PRICE > Double church: free; treasury:
€ 2.50; children under 13: free
INFO > Burg 13, tel. +32 (0)50 33 67 92,
www.holyblood.com

🦽 🖼 **02** **02** **04** Begijnhof (Beguinage)

The 'Princely Beguinage Ten Wijngaarde'
with its white-coloured house fronts,
tranquil convent garden and beguinage
museum was founded in 1245. This little
piece of world heritage was once the
home of the beguines, emancipated
lay-women who nevertheless led a pious
and celibate life. Today the beguinage is
inhabited by nuns of the Order of St.
Benedict and several Bruges women
who have decided to remain unmarried.
In the Beguine's house, you can still get a
good idea of what day-to-day life was like
in the 17th century.
OPEN > Beguinage: daily, 6.30 a.m.-
6.30 p.m.; Beguine's house: Monday to
Saturday, 10.00 a.m.-5.00 p.m.; Sunday
2.30 p.m.-5.00 p.m.
PRICE > Beguinage: free; Beguine's
house: € 2.00; 65+: € 1.50; children
aged 8 to 12 and students (on display of
a valid student card): € 1.00

INFO > Begijnhof 24-28-30, tel. +32 (0)50 33 00 11

05 09 Belfort (Belfry)

The most important of Bruges' towers stands 83 metres tall. It houses, amongst other things, a carillon with 47 melodious bells. In the reception area, (waiting) visitors can discover all kinds of interesting information about the history and working of this unique world-heritage protected belfry. Those who take on the challenge of climbing the tower can pause for a breather on the way up in the old treasury, where the city's charters, seal and public funds were kept during the Middle Ages, and also at the level of the impressive clock or in the carillonneur's chamber. Finally, after a tiring 366 steps, your efforts will be reward-ed with a breath-taking and unforget-table panoramic view of Bruges and its surroundings.

OPEN > Daily, 9.30 a.m.-6.00 p.m., last admission: 5.00 p.m. For safety reasons, only a limited number of persons will be allowed to visit the tower at the same time. Reservations are not possible. Each visitor has to wait in line. Please consider a certain waiting period.

ADDITIONAL CLOSING DATES > 1/1, 25/5 (1.00 p.m.-6.00 p.m.) and 25/12

PRICE > € 10.00; 65+ and youngsters aged 6 to 25: € 8.00; children under 6: free

INFO > Markt 7, tel. +32 (0)50 44 87 43, www.museabrugge.be

Bezoekerscentrum Lissewege – Heiligenmuseum (Visitors Centre Lissewege – Saints' Museum)

The Visitors Centre tells the story of 'the white village', which dates back through more than a thousand years of history. Unique photographs, maps, models, paintings and a collection of archaeological discoveries all illus-trate this glorious past. In the Saints'

Museum, you can admire a remarkable collection of more than 130 antique statues of patron saints.

OPEN > During the long weekend of 1 May (29/4 to 1/5), at weekends in May and June, during Ascension weekend (25/5 to 28/5), during Whit weekend (3/6 to 5/6), during the period 1/7 to 15/9 and in the last two weekends of September (16/9-17/9 and 23/9-24/9): 2.00 p.m.-5.30 p.m.

PRICE > Saints' Museum: € 2.00; children under 12: € 1.00

INFO > Oude Pastoriestraat 5, Lissewege, tel. +32 (0)495 38 70 95, www.lissewege.be; public transport: train Brugge-Zeebrugge

🐬 📶 Boudewijn Seapark Bruges

Welcome to the Boudewijn Seapark, where dolphins steal the show with their spectacular leaps and where sea lions and seals perform the craziest tricks. But it is not only the sea mammals in this family park that will charm you, but also the 20 outdoor park attractions that offer guaranteed fun for young and old alike. Finally, *Bobo's*

Indoor has 12 great indoor attractions, as well as *Bobo's Aqua Splash*, providing 1,100 square meters of wonderful water fun.

OPEN > During the period 1/4 to 1/10. During the Easter holidays (1/4 to 17/4) and weekends in April: 10.00 a.m.-5.00 p.m.; in May and June: daily, except on Wednesday, 10.00 a.m.-5.00 p.m.; in July and August: daily, 10.00 a.m.-6.00 p.m.; during the period 1/9 to 1/10: Saturday and Sunday, 10.00 a.m.-6.00 p.m. Please consult the website for details of the winter programme and the attractions that are open.

PRICE > All-in ticket: € 26.00; 65+ and children taller than 1 metre and under 12 years old: € 22.00; children between 85 cm and 99 cm: € 9.50; family ticket (2 adults + 2 children from 1 metre tall to 11 years of age): € 82.00

INFO > A. De Baeckestraat 12, Sint-Michiels, tel. +32 (0)50 38 38 38, www.boudewijnseapark.be. Tickets at the amusement park entrance or at the 🛈 tourist office 't Zand (Concertgebouw). Boudewijn Sea Park is situated just outside the city centre and is connected to the Bicycle Route Network; public transport: scheduled bus no. 7 or no. 17, bus stop: Boudewijnpark

NEW 📶 12 Brouwerij Bourgogne des Flandres (Brewery)

After an absence of 60 years, Bourgogne des Flandres is once again being brewed in Bruges. You can learn from the brewer himself how the beer is made, as well as tapping a digital glass

in the interactive space. Or perhaps you can have a bottle of the delicious brew personalized with your photo? The kids can enjoy themselves with a fun search game. And if you feel hungry or thirsty after your visit, why not sample something from the restaurant-bar, with its beautiful terrace overlooking the water.

OPEN > Tuesday to Sunday, 10.00 a.m.-6.00 p.m. and on all public holidays (including Mondays); last guided tour starts at 5.10 p.m.

PRICE > Including beer sampling: € 10.00; children aged 10 to 15: € 5.00 (without beer sampling); children under 10: free

LANGUAGES > Audio-guides are available in 9 languages: € 0.50

INFO > Kartuizerinnenstraat 6, tel. +32 (0)50 33 54 26, www.bourgognedesflandres.be

🔊 ⑬ Brouwerij De Halve Maan (Brewery)

The Halve Maan (Half Moon) is an authentic and historic brewery in the centre of Bruges. This 'home' brewery is a family business with a tradition stretching back through six genera-

tions to 1856. This is where the Bruges city beer – the *Brugse Zot* – is brewed: a strong-tasting, high-fermentation beer based on malt, hops and special yeast. In 2016 a unique underground beer pipeline, some 3 km long, was laid from the brewery in the city centre to the bottling plant in the suburbs. Daily tours of the brewery are organized, at the end of which visitors are offered a free glass of *Brugse Zot* blond beer.

OPEN > Sunday to Wednesday, 10.00 a.m.-6.00 p.m.; Thursday to Saturday, 10.00 a.m.-11.00 p.m. Guided tours: daily, on the hour, with the first tour at 11.00 a.m. and the last tour at 4.00 p.m. (5.00 p.m. on Thursday, Friday and Saturday)

ADDITIONAL CLOSING DATES > 1/1, 24/12 and 25/12

PRICE > Including refreshment: € 9.00; children aged 6 to 12: € 5.00; children under 6: free

LANGUAGES > English, Dutch, French. Other languages available on request.

INFO > Walplein 26, tel. +32 (0)50 44 42 22, www.halvemaan.be

📶 ⑮ Brugs Biermuseum (Bruges Beer Museum)

The top floor of the former post office building on the Markt is now the home of the Bruges Beer Museum. Using an iPad Mini you will discover the many fascinating facets of beer and the complexities of the brewing process (and that includes tasting!). What's more, you will learn all about Belgian – and Bruges – beer history, exploring the many different types and flavours of beer that our city and country produce. The kids' tour tells the fun story of the Bruges Bear.
OPEN > Daily, 10.00 a.m.-6.30 p.m., last admission: 5.00 p.m.
ADDITIONAL CLOSING DATES > 1/1 and 25/12
PRICE > Including iPad Mini (with headphones): € 15.00 (with 3 beer samplings) or € 9.00 (without beer samplings); children aged 5 to 15: € 5.00; children under 5: free; family ticket (2 adults + max. 3 children): € 32.00 (with beer sampling) or € 20.00 (without beer sampling)
LANGUAGES > iPad Minis are available in 10 languages
INFO > Breidelstraat 3 (former Post Office), tel. +32 (0)479 35 95 67, www.brugesbeermuseum.com

♿ 📶 03 07 ⑯ Brugse Vrije (Liberty of Bruges)

From this mansion, the countryside in a wide area around the city was once governed. The building functioned as a court of justice between 1795 and 1984. Today the city archives are stored here. They safeguard Bruges' written memory. The premises also boast an old assize court and a renaissance hall with a monumental 16th-century timber, marble and alabaster fireplace made by Lanceloot Blondeel.
OPEN > Daily, 9.30 a.m.-12.30 p.m. and 1.30 p.m.-5.00 p.m., last admission: 12.00 p.m. and 4.30 p.m.
ADDITIONAL CLOSING DATES > 1/1, 25/5 (1.00 p.m.-5.00 p.m.) and 25/12
PRICE > Including City Hall visit: € 4.00; 65+ and youngsters aged 12 to 25: € 3.00; children under 12: free. Tickets are sold in the town hall.
INFO > Burg 11A, tel. +32 (0)50 44 87 43, www.museabrugge.be

⑰ Choco-Story (Chocolate Museum)

The museum dips its visitors in the history of cocoa and chocolate. From the Maya and the Spanish conquistadores to

the chocolate connoisseurs of today. Children can explore the museum via a fun chocolate search game. Chocolates are made by hand and sampled on the premises. In 2015, the museum opened a thematic Choco-Jungle bar at Vlamingstraat 31, just a 5-minute walk away.

OPEN > During the period 1/9 to 30/6: daily, 10.00 a.m.-5.00 p.m., last admission: 4.15 p.m.; during the period 1/7 to 31/8: daily, 10.00 a.m.-6.00 p.m., last admission: 5.15 p.m.

ADDITIONAL CLOSING DATES >
1/1, 9/1 to 13/1 and 25/12

PRICE > € 8.00; 65+ and students: € 7.00; children aged 6 to 11: € 5.00; children under 6: free; several combination tickets possible *(see page 93)*

LANGUAGES > Audio-guides (included in the price) are available in German, Spanish, Italian and Japanese. The information panels are in English, French and Dutch.

INFO > Wijnzakstraat 2, tel. +32 (0)50 61 22 37, www.choco-story.be

♿ 🛜 ⑱ Concertgebouw – Open Huis (Concert Hall – Open House)

From September 2017, the Concert Hall will also be revealing its many fascinating secrets during the daytime. Let yourself be impressed by its stunning contemporary architecture and fantastic acoustics. Marvel at its remarkable art collection or even try your own hand at a little sound art. This original experience tour offers a unique behind-the-scenes view of the way a concert hall is run. There is a special version of the tour for children. During your visit, you will also learn more about the musical and artistic qualities of the Concert Hall.

OPEN > From September 2017: Wednesday to Saturday, 2.00 p.m.-6.00 p.m., last admission: 5.30 p.m.; Sunday, 10.00 a.m.-12.30 p.m., last admission: 12.00 p.m. Guided tours: Wednesday to Saturday at 3.00 p.m.

ADDITIONAL CLOSING DATES >
1/11, 11/11 and 25/12

PRICE > € 8.00; youngsters aged 6 to 26: € 4.00; children younger than 6: free

LANGUAGES > English, Dutch, French

INFO > 't Zand 34, tel. +32 (0)50 47 69 99, www.concertgebouw.be

Cozmix – Volkssterrenwacht (Public Observatory) Beisbroek

In the Cozmix observatory you will be

able to admire the beauty of the sun, moon and planets in glorious close-up, thanks to the powerful telescope. In the planetarium more than 7,000 stars are projected onto the interior of the dome. Spectacular video images take you on a journey through the mysteries of the universe: you will fly over the surface of Mars and pass through the rings of Saturn. The artistic planet-pathway (with sculptures by Jef Claerhout) will complete your voyage of discovery into outer space.

OPEN > Wednesday and Sunday, 2.30 p.m.-6.00 p.m.; Friday, 8.00 p.m.-10.00 p.m. Planetarium shows on Wednesday and Sunday at 3.00 p.m. and 4.30 p.m., on Friday at 8.30 p.m. During (Belgian) school holidays there are extra shows on Monday, Tuesday and Thursday at 3.00 p.m. and 4.30 p.m. Presentations in a foreign language are given on Wednesday at 4.30 p.m.: the first, third (and fifth) week of the month in French; the second and fourth week in English.
ADDITIONAL CLOSING DATES > 1/1 and 25/12
PRICE > € 6.00; youngsters aged 4 to 17: € 5.00
INFO > Zeeweg 96, Sint-Andries, tel. +32 (0)50 39 05 66, www.cozmix.be; public

transport: scheduled bus no. 52, no. 53 or no. 55, bus stop: Varsenare Velddreef. An approximate 20-minute walk from the bus stop.

⑲ Museum-Gallery Xpo Salvador Dalí

In the Cloth Halls, you can admire a fantastic collection of world-famous graphics and statues by the great artist Dalí. They are all authentic works of art that are described in the *Catalogues Raisonnés*, which details Salvador Dalí's oeuvre. The collection is presented in a sensational Daliesque décor of mirrors, gold and shocking pink.
OPEN > Daily, 10.00 a.m.-6.00 p.m.
ADDITIONAL CLOSING DATES > 1/1 and 25/12
PRICE > € 10.00; 65+ and students: € 8.00; children under 13: free
INFO > Markt 7, tel. +32 (0)50 33 83 44, www.dali-interart.be

㉒ Diamantmuseum Brugge (Bruges Diamond Museum)

Did you know that the technique of cutting diamonds was first applied in Bruges almost 550 years ago? The Bruges Diamond Museum tells this story in a

series of fascinating exhibition displays. And there is a live demonstration of diamond cutting each day – a memorable experience, not to be missed! In the diamond laboratory, microscopes and other equipment allow visitors, both young and old alike, to discover the true beauty of diamonds in all their many facets.

OPEN > Daily, 10.30 a.m.-5.30 p.m. Demonstrations: daily, 12.15 p.m.; during the weekends, (Belgian) school holidays and the period 1/4 to 31/10: extra demonstration at 3.15 p.m. (visitors need to be present 15 minutes in advance)

ADDITIONAL CLOSING DATES > 1/1, 9/1 to 20/1 and 25/12

PRICE > € 8.00 (without cutting demonstration) or € 11.00 (with cutting demonstration); 65+, students and children aged 6 to 12: € 7.00 (without cutting demonstration) or € 10.00 (with cutting demonstration); children under 6: free; family ticket (2 adults + 2 children): € 21.00 (without cutting demonstration) or € 24.00 (with cutting demonstration); a combi-ticket is possible *(see page 93)*

INFO > Katelijnestraat 43, tel. +32 (0)50 34 20 56, www.diamondmuseum.be

🛜 24 Foltermuseum De Oude Steen (Torture Museum)

De Oude Steen is one of the oldest prisons in Europe. The building has been renovated and transformed into a torture museum, with an extraordinary collection of artefacts and lifelike wax sculptures that shed a light on the controversial use of torture, where it was once thought that the end – justice – justified the means.

OPEN > During the period 1/7 to 15/9: daily, 10.30 a.m.-9.00 p.m.; during the period 16/9 to 30/6: daily, 10.30 a.m.-6.30 p.m.

ADDITIONAL CLOSING DAY > 25/12

PRICE > € 8.00; 60+: € 7.00; students: € 6.00; children under 6: free; family ticket (2 adults + 3 children under 16): € 20.00

INFO > Wollestraat 29, tel. +32 (0)50 73 41 34, www.torturemuseum.be

♿ 08 25 Frietmuseum (Belgian Fries Museum)

This didactical museum sketches the history of the potato, Belgian fries and the various sauces and dressings that accompany this most delicious and most famous of Belgian comestibles. The museum is housed in the Saai-

halle, one of Bruges' most attractive buildings. Show your entrance ticket and enjoy a € 0.40 discount on a portion of fries (in the basement).

OPEN > Daily, 10.00 a.m.-5.00 p.m., last admission: 4.15 p.m.
ADDITIONAL CLOSING DATES > 1/1, 9/1 to 13/1 and 25/12
PRICE > € 7.00; 65+ and students: € 6.00; children aged 6 to 11: € 5.00; children under 6: free; several combination tickets possible *(see page 93)*
INFO > Vlamingstraat 33, tel. +32 (0)50 34 01 50, www.frietmuseum.be

07 26 Gentpoort (Gate of Ghent)

The Gate of Ghent is one of four remaining medieval city gates. An entrance for foreigners, a border with the outside world for the townspeople of Bruges. The gate was a part of the city's defences as well as a passageway for the movement of produce and merchandise. Note the statue in the niche above the roadway: this is Saint Adrian, who was believed to protect the city during times of plague. The Ghent Gate is at its most beautiful in the evening, when it is quite literally in the spotlight.

OPEN > Saturday and Sunday, 9.30 a.m.-12.30 p.m. and 1.30 p.m.-5.00 p.m., last admission: 12.00 p.m. and 4.30 p.m.
ADDITIONAL CLOSING DAY > 1/1
PRICE > € 4.00; 65+ and youngsters aged 12 to 25: € 3.00; children under 12: free
INFO > Gentpoortvest, tel. +32 (0)50 44 87 43, www.museabrugge.be

27 Gezellemuseum (Gezelle Museum)

This literary and biographical museum about the life of Guido Gezelle (1830-1899), one of Flanders' most famous poets, was established in the house where he was born, situated in a peaceful working-class district of the city. In addition to displays about his life and works, there are also temporary presentations about (literary) art. Next to

the house there is a romantic garden, with Jan Fabre's *The Man Who Gives a Light* as the main attraction.

OPEN > Tuesday to Sunday, 9.30 a.m.-12.30 p.m. and 1.30 p.m.-5.00 p.m., last admission: 12.00 p.m. and 4.30 p.m. (open on Easter Monday and Whit Monday)

ADDITIONAL CLOSING DATES >
1/1, 25/5 (1.00 p.m.-5.00 p.m.) and 25/12

PRICE > € 4.00; 65+ and youngsters aged 12 to 25: € 3.00; children under 12: free

INFO > Rolweg 64, tel. +32 (0)50 44 87 43, www.museabrugge.be

♿ 📶 ㉘ Groeningemuseum (Groeninge Museum)

The Groeninge Museum provides a varied overview of the history of Belgian visual art, with the world-renowned Flemish primitives as a highlight. In this museum you can see, amongst other masterpieces, *Madonna with Canon Joris Van der Paele* by Jan van Eyck and the *Moreel Triptych* by Hans Memling. You will also marvel at the top 18th and 19th-century neoclassical pieces, masterpieces of Flemish Expressionism and post-war modern art.

OPEN > Tuesday to Sunday, 9.30 a.m.-5.00 p.m., last admission: 4.30 p.m. (open on Easter Monday and Whit Monday)

ADDITIONAL CLOSING DATES >
1/1, 25/5 (1.00 p.m.-5.00 p.m.) and 25/12

PRICE > Including Arentshuis: € 8.00; 65+ and youngsters aged 12 to 25: € 6.00; children under 12: free; a combination ticket is possible *(see page 93)*

INFO > Dijver 12, tel. +32 (0)50 44 87 43, www.museabrugge.be

㉙ Gruuthusemuseum (Gruuthuse Museum)

In the course of 2018, you will once again be able to admire this luxurious city palace of the lords of Gruuthuse in all its magnificent glory. After extensive restoration and renovation, visitors will once again be able to learn more about Bruges and enjoy the outstanding collections of tapestries, lace, sculpture, furniture and silver.

INFO > Dijver 17, tel. +32 (0)50 44 87 43, www.museabrugge.be

ℹ️ 🖼️ ♿ 📶 ㉚ Historium Bruges

Seven historically themed rooms, each complete with authentic decor, films and special effects, will take you back to a day in the year 1435. Follow the story of Jacob, an apprentice of Jan van Eyck, before later exploring the interactive exhibition and/or enjoying the panoramic view from the balcony over the Markt. The virtual reality spectacles of the VR Experience will immerse you in the day-to-day life of 15th century Brug-

es in a way you never imagined possible. Finish your visit in style in the Duvelorium Grand Beer Café.

OPEN > Daily, 10.00 a.m.-6.00 p.m., last admission: 5.00 p.m.

ADDITIONAL CLOSING DATE > 1/1

PRICE > Including audio-guide (available in 10 languages): € 13.50; students: € 10.00; children aged 3 to 12: € 7.50; VR Experience (13 years or older): an additional € 3.50; all-in ticket (visit Historium, VR Experience and a drink of your choice in the Duvelorium): € 19.00; family ticket (2 adults + 2 children): € 37.00; a combi-ticket is possible *(see page 93)*

INFO > Markt 1, tel. +32 (0)50 27 03 11, www.historium.be

♿ 32 Kantcentrum (Lace Centre)

Since 2014, the Lace Centre has been housed in the renovated old lace school of the Sisters of the Immaculate Conception. The story of Bruges lace is told in the lace museum on the ground floor. Multimedia installations and testimonies from international lace experts help to explain the various different types of lace and their geographical origin, as well as focusing on the lace industry and lace education in Bruges. In an interactive way, using touch screens, the visitor is introduced to the complexities of the 'spellenwerk': the making of lace with pins and bobbins. Demonstrations and various courses are organized in the lace workshop on the second floor. *(Also read the interview with Kumiko Nakazaki on pages 128-131.)*

OPEN > Monday to Saturday, 9.30 a.m.-5.00 p.m., last admission: 4.30 p.m. Demonstrations: Monday to Saturday, 2.00 p.m.-5.00 p.m.

ADDITIONAL CLOSING DATES > All (Belgian) public holidays

PRICE > € 5.20; 65+ and youngsters aged 12 to 26: € 4.20; children under 12: free; a combi-ticket is possible *(see page 93)*

INFO > Balstraat 16, tel. +32 (0)50 33 00 72, www.kantcentrum.eu

33 Lumina Domestica (Lamp Museum)

The museum contains the world's largest collection of lamps and lights. More than 6.000 antiques tell the complete story of interior lighting, from the torch and paraffin lamp to the light bulb and LED. The small detour into the world of

luminous animals and plants is particularly interesting. In this way you can discover, for example, the light mysteries of the glow-worm, the lantern fish and the small Chinese lantern.

OPEN > During the period 1/9 to 30/6: daily, 10.00 a.m.-5.00 p.m., last admission: 4.15 p.m.; during the period 1/7 to 31/8: daily, 10.00 a.m.-6.00 p.m., last admission: 5.15 p.m.

ADDITIONAL CLOSING DATES >
1/1, 9/1 to 13/1 and 25/12

PRICE > € 7.00; 65+ and students: € 6.00; children aged 6 to 11: € 5.00; children under 6: free; several combination tickets possible *(see page 93)*

INFO > Wijnzakstraat 2, tel. +32 (0)50 61 22 37, www.luminadomestica.be

♿ 🏠 15 35

Onze-Lieve-Vrouwekerk (Church of Our Lady)

The 115.5 metres high brick tower of the Church of Our Lady is a perfect illustration of the craftsmanship of Bru-

ges' artisans. The church displays a valuable art collection: Michelangelo's worldfamous *Madonna and Child*, countless paintings, 13th-century painted sepulchers and the tombs of Mary of Burgundy and Charles the Bold. The choir was renovated in 2015 and the remarkable church interior can now once again be admired in all its splendour.

OPEN > Monday to Saturday, 9.30 a.m.-5.00 p.m.; Sunday and Holy Days, 1.30 p.m.-5.00 p.m., last admission: 4.30 p.m. The church and the museum are not open to the public during nuptial and funeral masses. Useful to know: at the moment, large-scale renovation works are still being carried out, so the church is only partially accessible and many works of art cannot be viewed.

ADDITIONAL CLOSING DATES >
Museum: 1/1, 25/5 and 25/12

PRICE > Church: free. Museum: € 6.00; 65+ and youngsters aged 12 to 25: € 5.00; children under 12: free. There

is a discount on the entrance price during the renovation.
INFO > Mariastraat, tel. +32 (0)50 44 87 43, www.museabrugge.be

Onze-Lieve-Vrouw-Bezoe-kingkerk Lissewege (Church of Our Lady of Visitation)

The 13th-century brick Church of Our Lady of Visitation is a textbook example of 'coastal Gothic'. Its remarkable interior has a miraculous statue of the Virgin Mary (1625), an exceptional organ case and a beautifully sculptured rood loft and pulpit (1652). Anyone who makes the effort to climb all 264 steps of the squat, flat-topped tower will be rewarded with a panoramic view over the polders towards Ostend and Bruges.
OPEN > Church: daily, 10.00 a.m.-4.00 p.m.; during the period 1/5 to 30/9, 9.00 a.m.-6.00 p.m. Tower: 17/6-18/6, 24/6-25/6, 2/9-3/9, 9/9-10/9 and during the period 1/7 to 31/8, daily, 2.00 p.m.-5.30 p.m.
PRICE > Church: free. Tower: € 2.00; children under 12: € 0.50
INFO > Onder de Toren, Lissewege, tel. +32 (0)50 54 45 44 (church), +32 (0)487 49 92 14 (tower), www.lissewege.be; public transport: train Brugge-Zeebrugge

16 36 Onze-Lieve-Vrouw-ter-Potterie (Our Lady of the Pottery)

This hospital dates back to the 13th century, when nuns took on the care of pilgrims, travellers and the sick. In the 15th century, it evolved towards a more modern type of home for the elderly. The hospital wards with their valuable collection of works of art, monastic and religious relics and a range of objects used in nursing have been converted into a museum. The Gothic church with its baroque interior can also be visited.
OPEN > Tuesday to Sunday, 9.30 a.m.-12.30 p.m. and 1.30 p.m.-5.00 p.m., last admission: 12.00 p.m. and 4.30 p.m. (open on Easter Monday and Whit Monday)
ADDITIONAL CLOSING DATES > 1/1, 25/5 (1.00 p.m.-5.00 p.m.) and 25/12
PRICE > Church: free. Museum: € 4.00; 65+ and youngsters aged 12 to 25: € 3.00; children under 12: free
INFO > Potterierei 79B, tel. +32 (0)50 44 87 43, www.museabrugge.be

17 Onze-Lieve-Vrouw-van-Blindekenskapel (Chapel of our Lady of the Blind)

The original wooden Chapel of Our Lady of Blindekens was erected in 1305 as an expression of gratitude to Our Lady after the Battle of Mons-en-Pévèle (1304). The current chapel dates from 1651. In order to fulfil the 'Bruges promise', made on the field of battle, the Blindekens procession has paraded through the streets of the city on 15th August every year since 1305. As part of the procession, the women of Bruges donate a candle (of 18 kilograms) to the Church of Onze-Lieve-Vrouw-ter-Potterie.

OPEN > Subject to change: daily, 9.00 a.m.-5.00 p.m.
PRICE > Free
INFO > Kreupelenstraat 6

04 38 Expo Picasso

At the historic Oud Sint-Jan (Old St. John) site, you can view more than 400 original works of art by the great Spanish masters Pablo Picasso and Joan Miró. In addition to these permanent exhibitions, the 19th-century infirmary wards are also the setting each year for prestigious temporary expositions.

OPEN > Daily, 10.00 a.m.-6.00 p.m.
ADDITIONAL CLOSING DATES > 1/1, 9/1 to 3/2 and 25/12
PRICE > € 10.00; 65+ and youngsters aged 6 to 18: € 8.00; children under 6: free
INFO > Site Oud Sint-Jan, Mariastraat 38, tel. +32 (0)50 47 61 08, www.xpo-center-bruges.be

⌂ Seafront Zeebrugge

This maritime theme park, situated in the unique setting of the old fish market in Zeebrugge, allows you to explore the secrets of the Belgian fishing industry through the interactive exhibition 'Fish, from the boat right onto your plate' and discover the bustling world of the international port of Zeebrugge. The more restful visitors can enjoy the

story of coastal tourism past and present. Assume the role of the captain of the West-Hinder lightship or a sailor on a genuine Russian submarine. And don't forget to visit the large remembrance exhibition 'Besieged Coast, Occupied Harbour – Zeebrugge & WWI', as well as the new 'Fishtories' expo about the mysterious attraction of the sea and its allure for the men behind the fishing industry.

OPEN > During the period 1/9 to 30/6: daily, 10.00 a.m.-5.00 p.m.; during the period 1/7 to 31/8: daily, 10.00 a.m.-6.00 p.m; adapted opening hours in November and December: consult the website

ADDITIONAL CLOSING DATES > 1/1, 9/1 to 27/1 and 25/12

PRICE > Including visit to exhibitions: € 13.50; 60+ and students (on display of a valid student card): € 11.50; children under 12: € 9.50; children up to 1 metre (accompanied by an adult): free

INFO > Vismijnstraat 7, Zeebrugge, tel. +32 (0)50 55 14 15, www.seafront.be; public transport: train Brugge-Zeebrugge, from the station Zeebrugge-Dorp or Zeebrugge-Strand: coastal tram (direction: Knokke), stop: Zeebrugge-Kerk (Church)

19 Sint-Annakerk (St. Anne's Church)

This simple Gothic single-nave church, built in the 17th century, surprises with the opulence of its rich Baroque interior – the result of donations by wealthy local patrons. Admire the intricacy of the mar-ble rood-screen, the rich wooden panelling with inset confessional booths, the canvases of Jan Garemijn and the largest single painting in all Bruges.

OPEN > Subject to change: during the period 1/4 to 30/9: daily, 10.00 a.m.-1.00 p.m. and 2.00 p.m.-6.00 p.m.; during the period 1/10 to 31/3: daily, 2.00 p.m.-5.00 p.m. The church is not open to visitors during religious services.

PRICE > Free

INFO > Sint-Annaplein

20 Sint-Gilliskerk (St. Giles's Church)

In this church, the only one in the city centre with a tower clock, many of the great Bruges artists have been buried. These include Hans Memling, Lanceloot Blondeel and Pieter Pourbus. The church originally dates from the 13th century, but was extensively rebuilt in the 15th century. The exterior is a fine example of the robust Brick Gothic style, while the interior has a more refined 19th-century Neo-Gothic look.

OPEN > Subject to change: during the period 1/4 to 30/9: daily, 10.00 a.m.-1.00 p.m. and 2.00 p.m.-6.00 p.m.; during the period 1/10 to 31/3: daily, 2.00 p.m.-5.00 p.m. The church is not open to visitors during religious services.

PRICE > Free

INFO > Sint-Gilliskerkstraat

22 Sint-Jakobskerk (St. James's Church)

In the middle of the 13th century, the modest St. James's Chapel was elevat-

ed to the status of a parish church. During the 15th century, this simple house of prayer was extended to its current size. The church is now famous for its rich collection of art treasures, donated by wealthy local people living nearby, and for its fine examples of funerary art.

OPEN > Subject to change: during the period 1/4 to 30/9: daily, 10.00 a.m.-1.00 p.m. and 2.00 p.m.-6.00 p.m.; during the period 1/10 to 31/3: daily, 2.00 p.m.-5.00 p.m. The church is not open to visitors during religious services.

PRICE > Free

APP > You can visit the church using the Xplore Bruges app *(read more about the app on page 106).*

INFO > Sint-Jakobsplein

♿ 🛜 **39** Sint-Janshospitaal (Saint John's Hospital)

Saint John's Hospital has an eight hundred-year-old history of caring for pilgrims, travellers, the poor and the sick. Visit the medieval wards where the nuns and monks performed their work of mercy, as well as the church and the chapel, and marvel at the impressive collection of archives, art works, medical instru-

ments and six paintings by Hans Memling. Also worth a visit: the Diksmuide attic, the old dormitory, the adjoining custodian's room and the pharmacy.

OPEN > Museum: Tuesday to Sunday, 9.30 a.m.-5.00 p.m. Pharmacy: Tuesday to Sunday, 9.30 a.m.-12.30 p.m. and 1.30 p.m.-5.00 p.m., last admission both: 4.30 p.m. (both open on Easter Monday and Whit Monday)

ADDITIONAL CLOSING DATES > 1/1, 25/5 (1.00 p.m.-5.00 p.m.) and 25/12

PRICE > Including visit to the pharmacy: € 8.00; 65+ and youngsters aged 12 to 25: € 6.00; children under 12: free

APP > You can learn more about the six works of Hans Memling via the Xplore Bruges app *(read more about the app on page 106).*

INFO > Mariastraat 38, tel. +32 (0)50 44 87 43, www.museabrugge.be

40 Sint-Janshuismolen (Mill)

Windmills have graced Bruges' ramparts ever since the construction of the outer city wall at the end of the 13th century. Today four specimens are left on Kruisvest. The Sint-Janshuis Mill, built in 1770 and still occupying its original site, is the only mill still

grinding flour and the only mill open to visitors.

OPEN > During the period 1/4 to 30/9: Tuesday to Sunday, 9.30 a.m.-12.30 p.m. and 1.30 p.m.-5.00 p.m., last admission: 12.00 p.m. and 4.30 p.m. (open on Easter Monday and Whit Monday).

ADDITIONAL CLOSING DATE > 25/5 (1.00 p.m.-5.00 p.m.)

PRICE > € 3.00; 65+ and youngsters aged 12 to 25: € 2.00; children under 12: free

INFO > Kruisvest, tel. +32 (0)50 44 87 43, www.museabrugge.be

♿ 23 Sint-Salvators-kathedraal (Saint Saviour's Cathedral)

Bruges' oldest parish church (12th-15th century) has amongst its treasures a rood loft with an organ, medieval tombs, Brussels tapestries and a rich collection of Flemish paintings (14th-18th century). The treasure-chamber displays, amongst others, paintings by Dieric Bouts, Hugo van der Goes and other Flemish primitives.

OPEN > Cathedral: Monday to Friday, 10.00 a.m.-1.00 p.m. and 2.00 p.m.-5.30 p.m.; Saturday, 10.00 a.m.-1.00 p.m.

and 2.00 p.m.-3.30 p.m.; Sunday, 11.30 a.m.-12.00 p.m. and 2.00 p.m.-5.00 p.m.; the cathedral is not open to the public during masses. Treasury: daily (except Saturday), 2.00 p.m.-5.00 p.m. Useful to know: restoration work is currently being carried out in the cathedral. This can influence the opening hours of the treasure chamber.

ADDITIONAL CLOSING DATES > Cathedral (afternoon) and treasury (all day): 1/1, 25/5, 24/12 and 25/12

PRICE > Cathedral and Treasury: free

INFO > Steenstraat, tel. +32 (0)50 33 61 88, www.sintsalvator.be

42 Schuttersgilde Sint-Sebastiaan (Saint Sebastian's Archers Guild)

The Guild of Saint Sebastian is an archers' guild that has already been in existence for more than 600 years, which is unprecedented anywhere in the world. The members of this longbow guild are exclusively male, with two notable exceptions: Queen Mathilde of Belgium and the Queen of England. A visit includes the royal chamber, the chapel chamber and the garden.

OPEN > During the period 17/4 to 30/9:

Tuesday to Thursday, 10.00 a.m.-12.00 p.m. and Saturday, 2.00 p.m.-5.00 p.m.; during the period 1/10 to 16/4: Tuesday to Thursday and Saturday, 2.00 p.m.-5.00 p.m. Please note: do not be put off by the closed door; you always need to ring the bell to gain access.

ADDITIONAL CLOSING DATES >
17/6, 20/6 and 27/6
PRICE > € 3.00
INFO > Carmersstraat 174, tel. +32 (0)50 33 16 26, www.sebastiaansgilde.be

♿ 🛜 08 43 Stadhuis (City Hall)

Bruges' City Hall (1376) is one of the oldest in the Low Countries. It is from here that the city has been governed for more than 600 years. An absolute masterpiece is the Gothic Hall, with its late 19th-century murals and polychrome vault. In the historic chamber next door original documents and artefacts are used to evoke the history of the city's administration through the centuries. On the ground floor there is a free multimedia exhibition that illustrates the structural development of the Burg square and the City Hall.
OPEN > Daily, 9.30 a.m.-5.00 p.m., last admission: 4.30 p.m.

ADDITIONAL CLOSING DATES >
1/1, 25/5 (1.00 p.m.-5.00 p.m.) and 25/12
PRICE > Including Liberty of Bruges: € 4.00; 65+ and youngsters aged 12 to 25: € 3.00; children under 12: free
INFO > Burg 12, tel. +32 (0)50 44 87 43, www.museabrugge.be

🛜 45 Volkskundemuseum (Museum of Folk Life)

These renovated 17th century, single-room dwellings accommodate, amongst other things, a classroom, a millinery, a pharmacy, a confectionery shop, a grocery shop and an authentic bedroom interior. The upper floor is used for temporary exhibitions. You can relax in the museum inn, 'De Zwarte Kat' (The Black Cat) or in the garden,

where you can try out traditional folk games on the terrace.

OPEN > Museum and Inn: Tuesday to Sunday, 9.30 a.m.-5.00 p.m., last admission: 4.30 p.m. (open on Easter Monday and Whit Monday)

ADDITIONAL CLOSING DATES >
1/1, 25/5 (1.00 p.m.-5.00 p.m.) and 25/12

PRICE > € 4.00; 65+ and youngsters aged 12 to 25: € 3.00; children under 12: free; a combi-ticket is possible *(see below)*

INFO > Balstraat 43, tel. +32 (0)50 44 87 43, www.museabrugge.be

TAKE ADVANTAGE!

» Museum Pass

With the Museum Pass you can visit the different Musea Brugge locations (www. museabrugge.be) as often as you like for just € 20.00. Youngsters aged 12 to 25 pay just € 15.00. The pass is valid for three consecutive days and can be purchased at all Musea Brugge locations (except for the Liberty of Bruges) and at the 🛈 tourist office 't Zand (Concertgebouw).

» Combination ticket Historium/Groeninge Museum

Experience the Golden Age of Bruges in the Historium, with the painting of *Madonna with Canon Joris van der Paele* by Jan van Eyck as your leitmotif. Then see the masterpiece itself in the Groeninge Museum, along with the great works of many others of the so-called Flemish primitives. This € 17.50 combination ticket is only available in the Historium.

» Combination ticket Choco-Story/Diamond Museum

Combine a tasty visit to Choco-Story with a dazzling look at the Diamond Museum. This combination ticket costs € 17.00 (including diamond-cutting demonstration) or € 14.00 (without demonstration). For sale at the above-mentioned museums and at the 🛈 tourist office 't Zand (Concertgebouw).

» Combination ticket Choco-Story/Lumina Domestica/Belgian Fries Museum

Visit these three museums at reduced rates.

- » Combination ticket Choco-Story/Belgian Fries Museum: € 13.00; 65+ and students: € 11.00; children aged 6 to 11: € 8.00; children under 6: free
- » Combination ticket Choco-Story/Lumina Domestica: € 10.00; 65+ and students: € 9.00; children aged 6 to 11: € 7.00; children under 6: free
- » Combination ticket (3 museums): € 15.00; 65+ and students: € 13.00; children aged 6 to 11: € 10.00; children under 6: free. These combination tickets are for sale at the above-mentioned museums and at the 🛈 tourist office 't Zand (Concertgebouw).

» Combination ticket Lace Centre/Museum of Folk Life

Combination ticket: € 6.00, can only be purchased in either of these museums.

Culture and amusement

Concert Hall

The city's high-quality cultural life flourishes as never before. Devotees of modern architecture stand in awe of the Concertgebouw (Concert Hall) whilst enjoying an international top concert or an exhilarating dance performance. Romantic souls throng the elegant City Theatre for an unforgettable night. Jazz enthusiasts feel at home at Art Centre De Werf/Vrijstaat O, whereas the MaZ is the place to be for young people.

♿ 📶 **18** Concertgebouw (Concert Hall)

This international music and art centre is one of the *1001 buildings you must see before you die*. It is a place that offers the very best in contemporary dance and classical music. The impressive Concert Auditorium (1,289 seats) and intimate Chamber Music Hall (322 seats) are famed for their excellent acoustics. In the Concert Hall you can also admire various contemporary works of art.

INFO > 't Zand 34, tel. +32 (0)70 22 33 02 (ticket line: Monday to Friday, 4.30 p.m.-6.30 p.m.), www.concertgebouw.be

♿ **44** Stadsschouwburg (City Theatre)

The Bruges City Theatre (1869) is one of the best-preserved theatres of its kind in Europe and was fully restored in 2001. The sober neo-Renaissance facade of this royal theatre conceals a palatial foyer and an equally magnificent auditorium. This outstanding infrastructure is used for performances of contemporary dance and theatre and for concerts of various kinds.

INFO > Vlamingstraat 29, tel. +32 (0)50 44 30 60 (Tuesday to Friday, 1.00 p.m.-5.00 p.m. and Saturday 4.00 p.m.-7.00 p.m., closed 1/7 to 15/8), www.ccbrugge.be

♿ **34** Magdalenazaal (MaZ, Magdalena Concert Hall)

Its 'black-box' architecture means that the MaZ is the ideal location for youth events. The Bruges Cultural Centre and the Cactus Music Festival both organize pop and rock concerts here. Major artists from the world of music and more intimate club talents can all 'do their own thing' in the MaZ. Rising stars in the theatrical and dance arts also perform in this perfect setting. Children's and family events are regular features on the programme.

INFO > Magdalenastraat 27, Sint-Andries, tel. +32 (0)50 44 30 60 (Tuesday to Friday, 1.00 p.m.-5.00 p.m. and Saturday, 4.00 p.m.-7.00 p.m., closed 1/7 to 15/8), www.ccbrugge.be

21 De Werf/Vrijstaat O (Art Centre)

De Werf/Vrijstaat O. has an excellent and well-deserved reputation for jazz, dance, visual art and literature. From October to May, there is a free jam session on every second Monday of the month. De Werf/Vrijstaat O. is also an ideal location for staging plays and other podium performances. In short, it is a place that creates, presents and inspires.

INFO > Werfstraat 108, tel. +32 (0)50 33 05 29, www.dewerf.be

What's on the programme in 2017?

The list below shows some of the most important events taking place in Bruges. You can also find the same details in the monthly event calendar that you can pick up free of charge from the ℹ️ tourist information offices on the Markt (Historium), 't Zand (Concertgebouw) and in the Railway station. And, of course, for a detailed events calendar you can always consult the website at www.visitbruges.be.

Bach Academie

17/1/2017 – 22/1/2017

Bach learned his music at his mother's knee, but in 1705 he set off on foot to Lübeck to become an apprentice of Buxtehude, whose flawless piano technique and *Abendmusiken* concerts were without a doubt an enormous source of inspiration to the young Bach. The seventh Bruges Bach Academy explores the musical richness of the Protestant Reformation, with a focus on choral works.

INFO > www.concertgebouw.be *(You can read more about Bach and early music in the interview with Albert Edelman on pages 120-123)*

Brugs Bierfestival (Bruges Beer Festival)

4/2/2017 and 5/2/2017

For a whole weekend the courtyard of the Belfry, the city halls and the Market Square are the place to be for anyone who wants to learn more about Belgian beers, old and new! The festival brings together more than 80 Belgian breweries, which account for the production of more than 360 different beers.

INFO > www.brugsbierfestival.be

Wintervonken (Winter Sparks)

10/2/2017 and 11/2/2017

Winter Sparks brings warmth and conviviality to the Burg square. The fourth edition of this winter festival once again guarantees scintillating street theatre, atmospheric concerts and heart-warming fire installations.

INFO > www.wintervonken.be

B Major!

1/3/2017 – 5/3/2017

B Major! is a new biannual music festival in which all the professional musical actors in Bruges join forces. The result is an exciting five-day programme, specially made in the city for the city.

INFO > www.bmajor.be

More Music!

12/4/2017 – 15/4/2017

The Bruges Concert Hall and the Cactus Music Centre once again join forces to make More Music!, an exciting encounter between diverse and contrasting musical worlds. The result is an intriguing total concept that takes the visitor on an adventurous four-day voyage of musical discovery.

INFO > www.moremusicfestival.be

Mooov filmfestival

19/4/2017 – 27/4/2017

This film festival, screened in Cinema Lumière and Cinema Liberty, shows the best new films from Africa, Asia and South America. The programme covers both artistically innovative movies and films with a social conscience.

INFO > www.mooov.be

BruTaal

5/5/2017 – 14/5/2017

A new biannual literary festival that invites international writers to offer their own views of Bruges in words. You can discover the resulting stories, manifestos and 'urban legends' by following a special route that leads through the heart of the city.

INFO > www.brutaalbrugge.be

Meifoor (May Fair)

5/5/2017 – 28/5/2017

For three fun-filled weeks some 90 fairground attractions 'take over' 't Zand, the Beursplein, the Koning Albertpark and the Simon Stevinplein.

Memling in Context
A fresh look at Hans Memling's paintings of the Saint John's Hospital

11/5/2017 – 8/10/2017

The best way to learn about the masterpieces of Hans Memling, one of the greatest of the Flemish primitives, is to view them within the context of the wider collection of the St. John's Hospital. This new presentation sheds new light on his remarkably rich oeuvre.

INFO > www.museabrugge.be

CARILLON CONCERTS

Throughout the year, you can enjoy free, live carillon concerts in Bruges on Wednesdays, Saturdays and Sundays from 11.00 a.m. to 12.00 p.m. From mid-June to mid-September, evening concerts also take place on Mondays and Wednesdays from 9.00 p.m. to 10.00 p.m. The inner courtyard of the Belfry is a good place to listen.

INFO > www.carillon-brugge.be

Dwars door Brugge
(Running through Bruges)

May 2017

About 7,000 runners set off on a 15 km route through the city. This unique running event through the historic centre of Bruges is no longer just popular with local people, but now attracts competitors from all over the world. For the lesser gods, there is a 5 km course and a Kids Run is organized for children up to 12 years of age.

INFO > www.brugge.be

Budapest Festival

18/5/2017 – 20/5/2017

A three-day festival of music with concerts by the renowned Budapest Festival Orchestra, conducted by Iván Fischer.

A CENTURIES-OLD PROCESSION
25/5/2017

Every year on Ascension Day, under the watchful eye of a huge public, the Holy Blood Procession passes through the streets of Bruges city centre. In the first two parts of the procession, members of the religious community, various brotherhoods and numerous costumed groups play out well-known scenes from the Bible: from Adam and Eve in the Garden of Eden to the Passion of Christ. Next comes the story of Thierry of Alsace, Count of Flanders, who was awarded a few drops of the blood of Jesus by the patriarch of Jerusalem during the Second Crusade in 1146. This priceless relic was brought back to Bruges in a crystal bottle in 1150, since when believers have been able to revere the Holy Blood in the basilica of the same name. The final part of the procession is dedicated to the public veneration of the Holy Blood. Preceded by the Noble Fraternity of the Holy Blood, two prelates carry the reliquary through the city.

Each musical piece performed by Fischer and his orchestra gains a new dimension. Not surprisingly, the Budapest Festival Orchestra is regarded as one of the ten best orchestras in the world. A must for all music-lovers.
INFO > www.concertgebouw.be

Triatlon Bruges
June 2017
This quarter triathlon (1 km swimming, 45 km cycling and 10 km running) through the city centre and the area around Bruges is being organised for the 14th time this year. The event is exceptional because the swimming part takes place in the city's picturesque canals ('reien') and the athletes pass numerous famous tourist spots, such as the Rozenhoedkaai, the Dijver, the Burg, the Market Square, etc.
INFO > www.triatlonbrugge.be

Zandfeesten (Zand Festival)
2/7/2017
Flanders' largest antiques and second-hand market on 't Zand, the Beursplein and in the Koning Albertpark attracts bargain-hunters from far and wide.

Cactus Festival
7/7/2017 – 9/7/2017
This attractive open air festival in the Minnewater Park serves up a cocktail of rock, reggae, world music and electronica. Notwithstanding its international fame, the three-day festival manages to preserve a cosy and familial atmosphere, under its motto 'small is beautiful'. In addition to the concerts, plenty of attention is devoted to the fringe activities and there is also a wide range of food-and-drink options on offer.
INFO > www.cactusfestival.be

Moods!

28/7/2017 – 10/8/2017

For two whole weeks, there will be musical and other fireworks at unforgettable locations in Bruges city centre, such as the Belfry courtyard. In unique settings, you will be able to enjoy top national and international acts at one of the evening concerts. What's more, the concerts taking place on the Burg square are free.

INFO > www.moodsbrugge.be

MAfestival

4/8/2017 – 13/8/2017

Each year this highly respected festival of Ancient Music – MA stands for Musica Antiqua – continues to attract the world's top performers to Bruges and Bruges' Wood- and Wetland. In 2017, the MAfestival will turn the spotlight on Dante's iconic poem *La Divina Commedia*.

INFO > www.mafestival.be

(You can read more about early music in the interview with Albert Edelman on pages 120-123.)

Zandfeesten (Zand Festival)

6/8/2017

Flanders' largest antiques and second-hand market on 't Zand, the Beursplein and in the Koning Albertpark attracts bargain-hunters from far and wide.

Brugse Kantdagen (Bruges Lace Days)

9/8/2017 – 13/8/2017

Mid-August, the Walplein and the buildings of the Halve Maan Brewery buzz with lace activities: information and exposition stands, lace sale and demonstrations. Free entry.

INFO > www.kantcentrum.eu

(You read more about lace and the Lace Centre on page 85 and in the interview with Kumiko Nakazaki, pages 128-131.)

Benenwerk (Leg-work) – Ballroom Brugeoise

12/8/2017

Put your best leg forward for a festival that is guaranteed to bring out the dancer in you. Spread across various locations in Bruges city centre, you will be swept along by live bands and DJs for a dance marathon at no fewer than eleven different ballrooms, offering the most divergent dance music.

INFO > www.benenwerk.be

Lichtfeest (Festival of Light)

18/8/2017 and 19/8/2017

Lissewege, the 'white' polder village, once again wraps itself in a shroud of light and conviviality. As soon as the evening falls, you can enjoy atmospheric music, video art, street theatre, fire and light installations, etc. And all free of charge!

INFO > www.bruggeplus.be

Praalstoet van de Gouden Boom (Pageant of the Golden Tree)

19/8/2017 and 20/8/2017

The Pageant of the Golden Tree takes place every five years and is inspired by the festivities to celebrate the marriage of Charles the Bold and Margaret of York in 1468. The Golden Tree was the symbol

PIETER POURBUS AND THE FORGOTTEN MASTERS
13/10/2017 – 21/1/2018

During the second half of the 16th century, Bruges was hit by economic recession. The textile market stagnated and the foreign merchants left for home. Although the city maintained its international facade, many local people struggled to make financial ends meet. Ingenuity and creativity were the only weapons at their disposal. This was also true for artists like Pieter Pourbus, the members of the Claeissens family and Marcus Gerards. This exhibition focuses on the marketing choices made by these artists in their search for a new target group of potential customers. A selection of their unknown and half-forgotten masterpieces have been brought together to present a powerful image of the need for innovation in times of economic hardship.
INFO > www.museabrugge.be

of the chivalric tournament that was held on the Market Square as part of these celebrations. The modern day procession involves more than 2,000 costumed participants, several 'giants' and various decorated floats.
INFO > www.goudenboomstoet.be

Open Monumentendag (Open Monument Day)
9/9/2017 and 10/9/2017
During the second weekend of September, Flanders organises the 29th edition of Open Monument Day, when it opens the doors of its many monuments to the general public.
INFO > www.bruggeomd.be

Kookeet (Cook-Eat)
23/9/2017 – 25/9/2017
The seventh edition of Kookeet (Cook-Eat) will be organised in a stylish tented village at the rear of the station. During this three-day culinary event, thirty of

Bruges' gourmet chefs will serve various gastronomic dishes at fair prices.
INFO > www.kookeet.be

Zandfeesten (Zand Festival)
24/9/2017
Antiques and second-hand market on 't Zand, the Beursplein and in the Koning Albertpark.

Brugge Urban Trail
October 2017
The Bruges Urban Trail is a unique 10 km running event, taking in several of the city's beautiful parks and many of its important historic buildings. By running and jumping your way around the course, you will discover these tourist gems and magnificent monuments in a highly original manner!
INFO > www.sport.be/bruggeurbantrail

Iedereen klassiek (Everyone Classic)

28/10/2017

The classical music radio station Klara and the Concert Hall join forces to allow you to explore the beauty of Bach, Beethoven and the city of Bruges. This festival is traditionally brought to a close with a performance by the Brussels Philharmonic Orchestra, this year with a number of well-known pieces of Russian music.

INFO > www.concertgebouw.be

Razor Reel Flanders Film Festival

9/11/2017 – 14/11/2017

A feast of fun for the enthusiasts of fantastic films: from fairylike fantasies to frightening horror films, and from new releases to classics and genre cult films. In addition to film screenings, there are also workshops and exhibitions. The many guests will include celebrated national and international filmmakers.

INFO > www.rrfff.be

Christmas Market and ice-rink

End of November 2017 – beginning of January 2018

For more than a month, you can immerse yourself in the true Christmas atmosphere on the Market Square and at the Simon Stevinplein; on the Market Square you can even pull on your ice-skates.

December Dance

4/12/2017 – 17/12/2017

The annual rendezvous for dance-lovers from all over the world. Over a number of days, this festival brings together established names and young talent at a range of unique locations in the city. This year's guest curator is the French choreographer Christan Rizzo.

INFO > www.decemberdance.be

Bruges Christmas Run

December 2017

This unique running event (6 or 10 km) for charity celebrates its 7th edition in 2017. The course takes runners through the festively illuminated city centre and starts at 8.00 p.m. on the Market Square.

INFO > www.lopenvoorhetgoededoel.be

All dates are subject to possible change.

TRIENNIAL BRUGES 2018: LIQUID CITY

May 2018 – September 2018

In 2018, the Triennial will be coming to Bruges for the second time. Every three years, this artistic trajectory of contemporary art winds its way through the city, with installations by celebrated artists and architects dotted at a series of fascinating and often unexpected locations. The event not only shows Bruges quite literally as a 'liquid city', surrounded by water, but also figuratively, as a motor for social, cultural and political change. A place of diversity where people meet and a hotbed of new ideas and innovations. Sometimes a raging torrent, sometimes a babbling brook...

INFO > www.triennalebrugge.be

Huidenvettersplein

Tips from **Bruges experts**

Bruges: World Heritage city

Sonia Papili reveals
the Italian side of Bruges

During the week, the Italian Sonia Papili studies the North Sea with academic sobriety; during the weekend she guides her fellow countrymen with great passion around her adopted city. A passion that began gradually some eleven years ago, but now burns more brightly than ever.

ID-KIT

Name: Sonia Papili
Nationality: Italian
Date of birth: 17 May 1972
Living in Bruges since 2006. Sonia is a geologist with the Ministry of Defence and a tourist guide in Bruges.

Two geologists – him attached to the University of Ghent, her attached to the University of Rome – who met on a ship in Istanbul to discuss climate change: there are worse ways to start a long-distance relationship. For three years, the pair commuted back and forth between Italy and Belgium, before finally deciding to settle in Bruges.

'I had only been in Bruges once before,' says Sonia. 'I was much more familiar with Ghent, but my husband thought that Bruges better suited my personality and temperament. And he was right: Bruges really is my city!'

In the meantime, Sonia learnt Dutch and started work here as a geologist. During her citizenship programme, she became more and more curious about the history of her new home town. 'During the language course they told us a little bit about the history of the place. This intrigued me and so I decided to follow a three-year course to become an official guide in Bruges.'

'I was much more familiar with Ghent, but my husband thought that Bruges better suited my personality and temperament. And he was right: Bruges really is my city!'

WHY BRUGES IS A WORLD HERITAGE CITY

In 1998, the Bruges Beguinage was recognized as a World Heritage site. A year later, the Belfry received similar recognition. In 2000, this was extended to cover the entire city centre. Since 2009, the Holy Blood Procession has been listed as an item of immaterial World Heritage. Bruges also has a valuable and impressive architectural patrimony and is a fine example of an architecturally harmonious city. In particular, Bruges is famed for its Gothic style buildings in brick. In addition, its authentic and organically developed medieval urban fabric has been perfectly preserved and it is also the 'birthplace' of the Flemish primitives. In other words, reasons enough for UNESCO to label Bruges as a 'World Heritage city'.

Xplore
BRUGES
The Official City Tour App

XPLORE BRUGES – the official city tour app of Bruges

You can discover all the secrets of Bruges with the free Xplore Bruges-app. There are city walks, cycling circuits and indoor trails. Almost all the routes are available in five languages: English, Dutch, French, German and Spanish. At the moment, there are eleven different routes: from 'Bruges, anno 1562', through 'The hidden treasures of St. James's Church', to 'Handmade in Bruges'. In short, something for everyone!

Tip: download the app at home or from any wifi network, you no longer need access to mobile internet. If you are not familiar with downloading apps, check out the routes on the website www.xplorebruges.be.

Italian art

During her guide training Sonia soon discovered that she was not the first Italian to lose her heart to Bruges. From the 13th to the 15th century, Bruges was

an international trading centre that had close links with Europe's other great trading cities. This also meant with the great Italian cities, who around 1300 had decided to focus on international trade by sea as the best way to achieve fame and fortune, and saw Bruges as an ideal base for their activities in Northern Europe. Inspired by the success of the Italian merchants, the traders of other countries soon found their way to Bruges, which rapidly grew to become a northern counterpart to Venice. And so the 'Venice of the North' was born. 'A fine discovery for me, and one which made me look at the city – and in particular its Italian quarter – in a new light.' 'It is now widely known that the Italians traded here,' says Sonia, 'but they also left behind traces of their artistic heritage.' Sonia's thesis for her guide's training course dealt with the works of Italian art that can still be found in

Bruges. 'Of course, there is the *Madonna and Child* by Michelangelo in the Church of Our Lady, but there are many other Italian masterpieces to admire as well. I am thinking of the poetic *Veins of the Convent* by Giuseppe Penone in the Old St. John site. Or the three works by the contemporary artist Mario Molinari, who is famous in Italy, one of which is in the Kustlaan in Zeebrugge, near the old fish auction site. I also suspect that the beautiful medallions of Lorenzo de' Medici and his wife Clarice Orsini in the Bladelin Court were made in Italy, but I have found no evidence for this so far. What is beyond doubt is the fact that de' Medici, a family of 15th century Florentine bankers, did once run a bank from the Bladelin Court. I am also very impressed by the most recent statues on the facade of the City Hall. These were carved in the 1980s by Stefaan Depuydt (1937-2016) and his Italian wife, Livia Canestraro. Two of the statues are self-portraits of the couple. In fact, there are lots of places in Bruges where you can discover their work. They are a testimony to how beautiful and successful artistic collaboration between differing nationalities can sometimes be.'

Veins of the Convent

Starting young

Nowadays, Sonia passes on her love for Bruges to her former compatriots. 'Of course, the Italians love it when they are guided around the city in their own language. It is very often their first visit to Bruges, and because I understand them perhaps a little bit better than other guides, I can also show them a little bit more of the things that really interest them. Naturally, they first want to know what it's like to live here, about the schools and the medical system, about people's attitudes to work and leisure... With my hand on my heart, I can assure them that life here is really good.'

In the meantime, Sonia's own family also know where to find all the best places in Bruges. 'The city continues to evolve. As soon as anything new appears, I immediately want to check it out. In this way, my three daughters also get to share in my love of Bruges from an early age!'

(If you want to discover the beauty of Bruges with an official guide, please turn to page 68-69.)

Sonia Papili
Best addresses

FAVOURITE SPOT

» **Coupure**

'I am a big fan of the **Coupure**, a spot in the middle of the city but a million miles away from all the hustle and bustle. The way in which the majestic rows of trees draw a green line along Coupure Canal is pure art. What's more, our family is linked to the Coupure in a very special way.'

RESTAURANTS

» **Sans Cravate**, Langestraat 159, tel. +32 (0)50 67 83 10, www.sanscravate.be

'Our absolute favourite. Sans Cravate now has a star - and fully deserved. It's not somewhere we go every month, but if we have something special to celebrate, then we like to do it here! Chef Henk prepares both classic and contemporary dishes.'

» **De Schaar**, Hooistraat 2, tel. +32 (0)50 33 59 79, www.bistrodeschaar.be

'This is the perfect place for anyone who wants to enjoy to the full the Coupure - my favourite place in the city. In the summer, it's wonderful to just sit on a terrace at the water's edge; in the winter, you can enjoy the lovely open fire inside.'

» **De Bottelier**, Sint-Jakobsstraat 63, tel. +32 (0)50 33 18 60,
www.debottelier.com

'This is a real no-nonsense address with healthy cooking focused mainly on veg-
etables. And reasonably priced as well! Add to this a charming interior and you
will soon understand why the sign 'full' often hangs in the window.'

» **Du Phare**, Sasplein 2, tel. +32 (0)50 34 35 90, www.duphare.be

'After a pleasant summer walk along the ramparts or a climb up one of the
windmill hills, there is nothing nicer than getting your breath back on the large
sun terrace of Du Phare. And if the weather is not kind, you can enjoy the elegant
interior of this top-class bistro with its season-based, international cuisine.'

» **La Tâche**, Blankenbergse Steenweg 1, tel. +32 (0)50 68 02 52,
www.latache.be

'My husband went to eat here a few times and was always full of praise about the
food. The restaurant – housed in a beautiful city mansion – is known for its classic cooking, laced with the flavours of the South. That's why La Tâche is at the
top of my 'must visit' list.'

CAFÉS

» **De Proeverie**, Katelijnestraat 6,
tel. +32 (0)50 33 08 87,
www.deproeverie.be

'The best hot chocolate in Bruges
comes from this British-style tearoom.
Freshly melted chocolate with warm
milk: what more can you want? Perhaps something from their delicious
selection of homemade ice-creams,

cakes and scones! A visit to De Proeverie is always lip-licking good!'

» **Café Rose Red**, Cordoeaniersstraat 16, tel. +32 (0)50 33 90 51,
www.caferosered.com

'To be honest, I am not a big drinker, more a sipper and a taster. And there is no
better place to do this than in Café Rose Red, with its fine range of the very best
Belgian beers. They have dozens of them!'

» De Zolder, Vlamingstraat 53, tel. +32 (0)477 24 49 05

'A cellar cafe named 'De Zolder', which means 'attic' in Dutch: it could only happen in Belgium! De Zolder is a cool and relaxing café, where you can sample local beers in wonderful medieval surroundings. Ideal for a night-out with a group of friends.'

» De Belleman Pub, Jozef Suvéestraat 22, tel. +32 (0)50 34 19 89

'Local people affectionately call this traditional brown café on the corner of the Koningin Astridpark 'The Belleman's'. I love the classic British pub-atmosphere and the fact that you can chat to locals who have sat at the same place at the bar for years and years.'

» Grand Hotel Casselbergh, Hoogstraat 6, tel. +32 (0)50 44 65 00,
www.grandhotelcasselbergh.com

'The elegant bar of the Grand Hotel Casselbergh is a great place to chill out before or after your evening dinner. You can sit at the bar counter or lounge in one of the deliciously comfortable easy chairs. This is the place to start or round off your evening on the town in style. People not staying at the hotel are always more than welcome.'

SHOPPING LIST

» Callebert, Wollestraat 25,
tel. +32 (0)50 33 50 61,
www.callebert.be

'As a design freak, I can always find something to set my pulse racing at Callebert, a style oasis where timeless beauty reigns supreme. Complete with a children's department that will tempt the adults as well!'

» Da Vinci, Geldmuntstraat 34, tel. +32 (0)50 33 36 50, www.davinci-brugge.be

'It doesn't matter if the weather is freezing cold or boiling hot: there are always tourists lined up in droves outside this deluxe ice-cream parlour. The number of different flavours is almost beyond belief. What's more, everything – from the ice-cream right down to the sauces – is made on the premises.'

» **Krokodil**, Sint-Jakobsstraat 47, tel.
+32 (0)50 33 75 79, www.krokodil.be

'A regular port-of-call for people with
kids. This not the place for 'throw-
away' junk, but for beautiful and solidly made toys that will stand the test
of time.'

» **De Witte Pelikaan**, Vlamingstraat 23,
tel. +32 (0)50 34 82 84, www.dewittepelikaan.be

'Whoever loves Christmas will love De Witte Pelikaan, with its year-round selection of Christmas baubles and jingle bells.'

» **BbyB**, Sint-Amandsstraat 39, tel. +32 (0)50 70 57 60, www.bbyb.be

'At BbyB you can find a range of elegantly sleek haute couture chocolates that
are almost impossible to resist. Time after time I am tempted by this classy concept store to try out new and exciting flavour combinations. Because let's admit
it: who can say 'no' to chocolate with rhubarb, speculoos biscuit, 'babulettes' or
star aniseed?'

SECRET TIP

» **The remains of the old
St. Donatian Cathedral**, Burg 10,
tel. +32 (0)50 44 68 44

'Under the prestigious Crowne Plaza Hotel lay hidden the remains of
the **St. Donatian Cathedral**, which
during the Middle Ages represent-
ed the ecclesiastical power of
the Church on the Burg square.
St. Donatian's was the court church of the counts of Flanders and therefore the
most important church in Bruges. If you really want to dig into the oldest parts of
the city's historic past, ask at the reception desk if you can take a look in their
cellar. Because in Bruges, the ground is always full of history.'

Flemish primitives in the spotlight

Till-Holger Borchert sees respect
as the key to succes

He was born in Hamburg, he lives in Brussels and he thoroughly enjoys
his work in Bruges as he finds himself surrounded by six centuries of
fine arts, and especially the magnificent masterpieces of the Flemish
primitives. In 2002, Till-Holger Borchert was one of the curators of
Bruges, Cultural Capital of Europe. Today he is chief curator of the
Groeninge Museum and the Arentshuis.

ID-KIT

Name: Till-Holger Borchert
Nationality: German
Date of birth: 4 January 1967
This chief curator of the Groeninge Museum lives
in Brussels but works in Bruges. He is the author of
countless publications on the Flemish primitives.

'Bruges is an exceptionally beautiful city,' says Till-Holger Borchert. 'What's more, it is also a wonderfully liveable place, partly because of the clever and careful way in which the city has been able to mix her medieval character with a modern ambiance. As early as the 13th century, the concentration of wealthy citizens enabled Bruges to become the commercial heart of North-western Europe. In the 15th century, the Burgundian authorities took successful structural measures, which resulted in an increase of the population and had a positive effect on the city's further development. Just as importantly, Bruges was spared the many ravages of the so-called Iconoclastic Fury, which caused so much damage in other cities. That spirit of respect and tolerance still pervades the city today. I must say it is a great joy to be here. The countless locals and visitors will surely fully agree with me.'

Madonnas from around the Corner

'Nearly every day I go and greet two masterpieces: Hans Memling's *Madonna*

MUSEUM SHOP

'Whoever enters the museum shop of the Groeninge Museum will leave with some wonderful memories, that I can assure you. Perhaps you will take home your favourite art treasures in the shape of a handsomely illustrated book or a reproduction on a poster maybe, or depicted on a few picture postcards. And why don't you surprise yourself with an original souvenir? I have caught not only some of my delighted fellow curators buying just such a present for themselves, but my wife as well!'

and Maarten van Nieuwenhove at the Saint John's Hospital and Jan van Eyck's *Madonna with Canon Joris van der Paele* at the Groeninge Museum. I am not saying that I discover something new every time I look at them, but my curiosity and my pleasure remain as great as ever.

And I still try and find out new things about them. They just continue to fascinate me! I sometimes wonder why people from all corners of the world have always found the Flemish primitives so absorbing. The answer perhaps lies in the fact that for the very first time in art history we are confronted with recognisable people and familiar objects that correspond to today's reality. Even a Madonna seems to look like the woman from around the corner. The Flemish primitives laid the foundation of an artistic concept that in its realism is perfectly recognisable and therefore understandable to a modern-day observer. The Flemish primitives discovered the individual. Quite a feat. Those Flemish painters were also dab hands at solving the problems. They explored space in an incredibly skilful and sophisticated way, for example by placing a mirror somewhere in the room. In Memling's diptych, a round mirror on the left-hand side behind the Madonna reflects the interior

*'Nearly every day I go
and greet two masterpieces.'*

she is sitting in. In it, her own portrait is painted just a whisker away from the silhouette of the patrician Maarten van Nieuwenhove, Memling's patron. Truly magnificent. Are these works of art still capable of moving me? Absolutely. For pure emotion a painter like Rogier van der Weyden touches me more deeply than Jan van Eyck. The works of van Eyck or Memling impress me more with their intellectual and conceptual qualities. Van der Weyden and van Eyck: it is worth visiting the treasure houses of Bruges, even if only for the pleasure of enjoying these two opposite ends of the artistic spectrum.'

INTERESTING TOMBS

The central feature in the Jerusalem Chapel – located in the Saint-Anne district – is the ceremonial tomb of Anselm Adornes (1424-1483) and his wife, Margareta Vander Banck (d. 1462). Anselm – scion of a wealthy merchant family, confidant of the dukes of Burgundy and a counsellor of the King of Scotland – had this chapel built in the likeness of the Church of the Holy Sepulchre in Jerusalem, with the intention that he should be buried here with his spouse. However, Anselm was killed and buried in Scotland. Only his heart was later added to the tomb in Bruges. The decorative tombstone depicts Anselm and Margareta 'en gisant': lying stretched out with their heads on a cushion and their hands folded in prayer. Anselm is dressed as a knight, with a lion at this feet, symbolizing courage and strength. Margareta is dressed as a noblewoman; at her feet rests a dog, symbolizing faithfulness.

Till-Holger Borchert
Best addresses

FAVOURITE SPOT

» The churches of Bruges

'The great churches of Bruges possess wonderful art collections, containing pieces that wouldn't disgrace any top-flight museum. Look up at the sheer breathtaking height of the Church of Our Lady, whose 115.5-metre high tower is the second tallest brick-built tower in the world. When in Saint Saviour's, do go and marvel at the frescoes in the baptistery. And Saint-James's Church is worth its while for the impressive **mausoleum of the de Gros family**, because this sculptural masterpiece reveals par excellence the self-confidence and power of the Burgundian elite.'

RESTAURANTS

» Rock-Fort, Langestraat 15,
   tel. +32 (0)50 33 41 13,
   www.rock-fort.be

'Rock-Fort serves original, contemporary dishes with a modern twist. Their cooking is so good that the place is packed all week long. Local people love it, and I also like to pop in from time to time. But be careful: it is closed during the weekends.'

» Den Amand, Sint-Amandsstraat 4, tel. +32 (0)50 34 01 22,
   www.denamand.be

'In Den Amand I once saw a German restaurant critic copy out the entire menu card. You can't get higher praise than that! A small and elegant bistro, where you will find both tourists and local people enjoying the excellent food.'

» **'t Schrijverke**, Gruuthusestraat 4, tel. +32 (0)50 33 29 08, www.tschrijverke.be
'This homely restaurant is named after a poem by Guido Gezelle, which hangs in
a place of honour next to the door. But 't Schrijverke is above all rightly famed for
its delicious regional dishes and its *Karmeliet* beer on tap.'

» **Tanuki**, Oude Gentweg 1, tel. +32 (0)50 34 75 12, www.tanuki.be
'A true temple of food, where you immediately drop your voice to the level of a whis-
per, so that you don't disturb the silent enjoyment of the other diners. In the open
kitchen the chef does magical things with sushi and sashimi, and prepares his
seven course menus with true oriental serenity.'

» **Den Gouden Harynck**, Groeninge 25, tel. +32 (0)50 33 76 37,
  www.goudenharynck.be
'Den Gouden Harynck is a household name in Bruges, known and loved by foodies of all kinds. It is also one of the most pleasant star-rated restaurants in the
city – as anyone who has ever been there will tell you.'

CAFÉS

» **Café 't Klein Venetië**, Braamberg-
  straat 1, tel. +32 (0)50 33 10 37
'Every Bruges local knows that if you
want to enjoy the sun, the terrace of
Café 't Klein Venetië is the best place to
come. I like to sit here on the front row,
enjoying the busy crowds on the Huidenvettersplein and the magnificent
view over the Rozenhoedkaai, the most

photographed spot in Bruges. In short, when you are on this super-popular terrace, you never know where to look first. '

» **Delaney's Irish Pub & Restaurant**, Burg 8, tel. +32 (0)50 34 91 45,
  www.delaneys.be
'It's always party time in this Irish pub, with its distinctive international atmosphere. Delaney's is the kind of place where you can rub shoulders with the whole
world at the bar.'

» The Druid's Cellar, Sint-Amandsstraat 11, tel. +32 (0)50 61 41 44, www.thedruidscellar.eu

'I like to drop in at The Druid's Cellar every now and again, even if only to watch Drew, my favourite barkeeper, in action. Or simply to relax and enjoy a glass from their wide range of Scottish and Irish whiskies. They always taste just that little bit better in The Druid's.'

» Café Marcel, Niklaas Desparsstraat 7-9, tel. +32 (0)50 33 55 02, www.hotelmarcel.be

'Café Marcel is Bruges' refined version of a contemporary vintage café. In other words, a café from the days of yesteryear, but in a tight, new design setting. Think of dark wooden floorboards, simple lamps, leather benches and original wood panelling. You can pop in here for a tasty breakfast or an aperitif with tapas.'

» Hollandse Vismijn, Vismarkt 4, tel. +32 (0)50 33 33 01

'Whenever I fancy one of the popular Belgian beers, you will probably find me in the Hollandse Vismijn. This cheap and cheerful 'people's pub' is on the Fish Market. It is the type of café where everybody knows everybody and where you always get a warm welcome. Cheers!'

SHOPPING LIST

» Antiquariaat Van de Wiele,
Sint-Salvatorskerkhof 7,
tel. +32 (0)50 33 63 17,
www.marcvandewiele.com

'For art and history I was fortunate enough to discover Marc Van de Wiele Antiques. This is undoubtedly one of the best addresses in a city that is rich in antique shops. The place to find unique, illustrated books from days long gone by.'

» Boekhandel De Reyghere, Markt 12, tel. +32 (0)50 33 34 03, www.dereyghere.be

'For all my other reading material I rely on De Reyghere, located on the Market Square. Foreign visitors feel instantly at home in this book and newspaper store, primarily because of the large number of international titles it has on sale.'

» **Den Gouden Karpel**, Vismarkt 9-10-11, tel. +32 (0)50 33 33 89,
www.dengoudenkarpel.be

'The fishing family Ameloot have been running Den Gouden Karpel with heart and soul for many years: not only an excellent catering service and fishmongers, but also a top-class fish bar, where you can enjoy the fruits of the sea at their very best. For a fish-lover like myself, it is hard to walk past Den Gouden Karpel without stopping to buy something.'

» **D's Deldycke traiteurs**, Wollestraat 23, tel. +32 (0)50 33 43 35,
www.deldycke.be

'In the 15th century the Spaniard Pedro Tafur was already praising Bruges for its wide available selection of exotic fruits and rare spices. The Deldycke caterer is proud to continue this centuries-old tradition. Here, all your culinary wishes will be fulfilled.'

» **Parallax**, Zuidzandstraat 17, tel. +32 (0)50 33 23 02, www.parallax.be

'I always buy my socks at Parallax, but they are also experts at stylishly camouflaging my beer belly! Highly recommended for other fashion victims and the vestimentally challenged! Boss, Scabal, Zilton, Falke: you can find them all here.'

SECRET TIP

» **Museumshop**, Hof Arents, Dijver 16,
www.museabrugge.be

» **Jerusalem Chapel**, **Gezelle Museum**,
Lace Centre, **Church of Our Lady of
the Pottery** and **Museum of Folk Life**:
*see pages 74, 83-84, 86-87 and 92-93
for more information.*

'Whenever I want to take a breather, I saunter down Saint Anne's, Bruges' most striking working-class neighbourhood. You can still sense the charm of an authentic community in the streets around the **Museum of Folk Life**. The area boasts many fascinating places, too. Off the cuff, if I may: Our Lady of the Pottery, the Lace Centre, the medieval Jerusalem Chapel and the Gezelle Museum.'

Cultural capital Bruges
Albert Edelman
fills the Concert hall

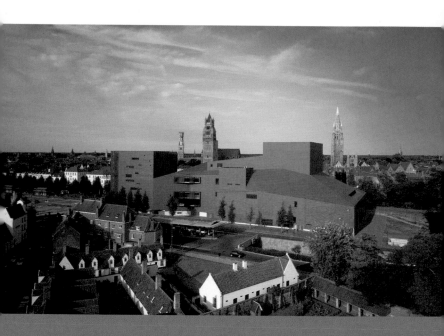

Each year, the Bruges Concert Hall continues to attract an increasingly bigger and more diverse audience, and this is partly the merit of Albert Edelman. As artistic coordinator for Early Music, he manages to lure the very best ensembles to Bruges; a matter, he says, of pleasing both the local people and the tourists musically.

ID-KIT

Name: Albert Edelman
Nationality: Dutch
Date of birth: 3 October 1978
Has lived in Bruges since 2011. Albert is artistic
coordinator for Early Music at the Concert Hall.

The Belgians and the Dutch may speak the same language, but that does not necessarily mean they always understand each other. Albert Edelman discovered this for himself in 2011, when he exchanged the Early Music Festival in Utrecht, the Netherlands, for a job as artistic coordinator for Early Music at the Bruges Concert Hall. 'During the first weeks, I really had difficulty understanding people. When my local baker spoke to me each morning, I just stood there with a smile. But that's all behind me now. Flemish people think a bit longer before saying something, and I like that. There is also more distance between people here than is customary in the Netherlands. The locals in Bruges need more time to get to know someone, which is not a bad thing, and I love that. Yes, I like it here a lot.'

In the meantime, Albert now feels fully at home in Bruges and each morning, just like his fellow citizens, he cycles cheerfully to his work. 'I live near the Sint-Anna canal, so my 'commuting' is extremely picturesque. A beautiful panoramic picture, with the Bruges Belfry as one of the highlights: 83 metres tall and comprising 47 bells, 27 tons of bronze and more than 500 years of carillon history.'

Different styles, no compromises

Add to this a varied, challenging job and my joy is complete! There are relatively few concert halls that pay as much attention to 'my' kind of music as the Bruges Concert Hall. Right from the very beginning, it was clear that early and contemporary music would both have a place here. This results in a very diverse programme; we bring a multiplicity of different styles, but we always try to tell a story with what we offer. In my opinion, music played on old instruments truly belongs in a historical city like Bruges: it is like an echo of what once has been. What's more, the musical opportunities offered by the Concert Hall itself are outstanding; its acoustics are absolutely

'You can also see that a long cultural tradition already exists in Bruges. This leads to an exciting interaction.'

top-draw. We can present all different kinds of genres, from chamber music to a capella, without having to compromise. Everything sounds good in the Concert Hall. Technically, the sound quality is always perfect, which is very unusual. In short, this is the place where you can enjoy music and dance in the best possible circumstances.'

And Albert also does plenty of enjoying of his own: 'I know less about contemporary music and dance, which is why I am making grateful use of my stay in Bruges to discover the delights of these genres.' Fortunately, a lot of other culture lovers share his views. 'We have a very good and loyal public. People who are curious, who want to hear new things and follow our tips. We work with reasonable ticket prices, so that we can reach a wider audience. In the foyer before a performance you will see distinguished gentlemen in suits rubbing shoulders with young people in jeans. Everyone feels welcome here, whether they are local people or tourists. People genuinely come for the music – and not to be seen – which really pleases me.'

'You can also see that a long cultural tradition already exists in Bruges. This leads to an exciting interaction. We challenge the audience, and in return they let

THE MUSICAL EVENT LIST OF ALBERT EDELMAN

1. 'The **Bruges MAfestival** is one of the world's most famous festivals for Early Music. For ten days, a surprising range of concerts is organised at different locations in the city and its immediate surroundings. In addition, there are also numerous readings, workshops and master classes.'
    (For more information about the MAfestival see page 99.) www.mafestival.be

2. 'The **Bach Academie**, in collaboration with Philippe Herreweghe, has become a firm favourite with Bach lovers all over the world. About 30% of the visitors come from abroad. Each year, the festival weekend attracts leading international musicians and ensembles, who specialize in the incomparable oeuvre of Johann Sebastian Bach.' *(For more information about the Bach Academy see page 96.)* www.concertgebouw.be

3. 'The **concerts of Anima Eterna Brugge**. This fantastic orchestra explores the classic, Romantic and early modern repertoire. They perform on historical instruments and with great respect for the original intentions of the composer.' www.animaeterna.be

BRUGES AND THE CARILLON:
A SHARED HISTORY

The very first bells were developed in China, around 2000 B.C. The art of bell-making was then brought to the Roman Empire via Egypt and Greece, and from there arrived in Northern Europe around 400 A.D. Bells were soon used as a means to call the faithful to prayer and to warn the population of approaching danger. Charlemagne made the use of bells in a belfry obligatory at the end of the 8th century. Towards the end of the 13th century, bells were attached to mechanical mechanisms for the first time. In the 16th century, rich cities like Bruges added grandeur to their belfries and church towers by adding more and more bells. And so the carillon - the oldest (and biggest) musical mass medium in history - was born! In the 17th century, the technique was refined and since the 18th century the carillon, which officially must have at least 23 bells, has functioned as an independent musical instrument. Since the beginning of the 20th century, the art of carillon playing has undergone international expansion. In November 2014, UNESCO recognized Belgian carillon culture as an intangible item of world cultural heritage. The Bruges Belfry boasts a triumphal bell from 1680, which is two metres in diameter and weighs 6 tons. The bells in the current carillon largely date from the 18th century and were recently renovated. For more than 500 years, bell music has rung out across the city. On Monday and Wednesday evenings in summer, the free concerts attract lots of people to the inner courtyard of the Belfry. The carillon also plays every Wednesday, Saturday and Sunday from 11.00 a.m. to 12.00 p.m.

us know what they want to hear and see.' In order to keep that audience captivated, Albert regularly goes on reconnaissance trips. 'I have the opportunity to see and hear many new things, both here and abroad. In this way, I keep up to date with everything happening in the music world. By meeting other musicians, it is possible to make plans together, which in turn often leads to unique custom-written programmes that are mainly performed in Bruges. In addition, I am constantly searching for young, fresh talent. Many young people are active in music from the Middle Ages, the Renaissance and the Baroque period, so there are plenty of new initiatives. In my mind, there is no doubt: Early Music is alive and kicking, more so than ever before! And certainly in Bruges!'

Albert Edelman
Best addresses

FAVOURITE SPOT

» **Sint-Janshospitaal (St. John's Hospital)**, Mariastraat 38, tel. +32 (0)50 44 87 43, www.museabrugge.be

'The **St. John's Hospital** does not display too many pieces, so that attention can be focused on the six Memlings in the collection. The impressive attic is ideal for performances and exhibitions.' *(See also pages 90 and 97)*

RESTAURANTS

» **Bhavani**, Simon Stevinplein 5, tel. +32 (0)50 33 90 25, www.bhavani.be

'A little piece of Bombay in the Simon Stevin Square. Here you can enjoy the more refined Indian cooking, whether in summer on the terrace or in winter around the cosy open fire. And Ganesh saw that it was good.'

» **Bistro Bruut**, Meestraat 9, tel +32 (0)50 69 55 09, www.bistrobruut.be
'In a short space of time, this place has become a reference for every Bruges foodie. In here, you can enjoy a delicious meal in a simple setting with a relaxed atmosphere. Top gastronomy without frills.'

» **Refter**, Molenmeers 2, tel. +32 (0)50 44 49 00, www.bistrorefter.com
'Whoever wants to eat gastronomically without paying astronomically is definitely at the right address. What's more, this affordable bistro owned by top chef Geert Van Hecke has a heavenly terrace.'

» Bistro Christophe, Garenmarkt 34, tel. +32 (0)50 34 48 92,
www.christophe-brugge.be

'This evening and night bistro serves French classics and seasonal suggestions until the early hours. Ideal for anyone who wants a nice dinner after a show.'

» Osteria 45, Sint-Jakobsstraat 45, tel. +32 (0)50 69 83 07, www.osteria45.be

'Osteria 45 not only serves richly topped pizzas and fresh-made pasta, but you can also get delicious cocktails, which makes the wait for your meal even more enjoyable. The service is not typically Bruges – but typically Italian with singing!'

CAFÉS

» Groot Vlaenderen, Vlamingstraat 94,
tel. +32 (0)50 68 43 56,
www.grootvlaenderen.be

'A cocktail bar with the air of a chic hotel lobby. A place that could just as easily be found in Hong Kong or New York. On top of that, the cocktails are perfect and the seats incredibly comfortable.'

» Craenenburg, Markt 16, tel. +32 (0)50 33 34 02, www.craenenburg.be

'The Craenenburg is rightly proud of its unique terrace. It is also the best place to hear the Belfry, Bruges' greatest and most beautiful musical instrument, in all its glory.'

» Concertgebouwcafé, 't Zand 34, tel. +32 (0)50 47 69 99,
www.concertgebouw.be/cafe

'Of course, it is impossible for me to exclude the Concert Hall café from this little list. It's the perfect place to hang out before and after shows. You can also pop in during the day to order one of the suggestions or just have a coffee.'

» De Republiek, Sint-Jakobsstraat 36, tel. +32 (0)50 73 47 64,
www.cafederepubliek.be

'The Republiek recently rose, phoenix-like, from its ashes and now boasts a brand new interior. Fortunately, the huge walled inner courtyard remains unchanged. A pleasant spot to sit and chat, or simply to enjoy the sun.'

» Monsieur Ernest, Wulfhagestraat 43, tel. +32 (0)50 96 09 66,
www.monsieurernest.com

'The privileged location of this outstanding hotel bar is enough to make everyone's mouth water. Nervous about going inside? There's no need to be: non-
hotel guests are always more than welcome. It is the best way to enjoy the
Bruges canals in style!'

SHOPPING LIST

» Le Pain de Sébastien, Smedenstraat 31, tel. +32 (0)50 34 47 44,
www.lepaindesebastien.be

'There is bread and bread. Only the
best ingredients are good enough for
Sébastien Cailliau, and you can taste
that in every bite. This explains why
you always have to queue here every
Saturday.'

» Café Costume, Ezelstraat 10, tel. +32 (0)50 66 11 98, www.cafecostume.com

'Trendy and timeless made-to-measure suits of the very highest quality and tail-
oring skill. That is the trademark of Café Costume. From the basic material to
the lining and the cufflinks: you decide it all. The result is a garment that is truly
unique. Sometimes rock 'n roll, sometimes classic - but always with an exclusive twist.'

» Vero Caffè, Sint-Jansplein 9, tel.+32 (0)50 70 96 09

'This is the best address for anyone who really likes coffee. Add a rich choice of
teas and fresh, home-baked cakes and pastries, and my happiness is complete.'

» De Corte, Sint-Amandsstraat 28, tel. +32 (0)50 33 46 07, www.decortebrugge.be

'From students to businessmen: everyone finds their way to De Corte. It is the
address in Bruges for original, affordable yet top-quality pens, leatherware and
accessories. If you ever want to buy that exclusive Montblanc or a moleskin
notebook, this is the place to come.'

» **Rombaux**, Mallebergplaats 13,
   tel. +32 (0)50 33 25 75,
   www.rombaux.be

'Music fans can indulge themselves
here to their heart's content. Browse
through scores, pick out CDs or admire
the wonderful interior; all is possible in
Rombaux.'

SECRET TIP

» **Lissewege**

'I live in the Saint-Anne district, a lovely place, but **Lissewege** is also highly
recommended. Each time the MAfestival takes place, you can find me there.
Thanks to the impressive acoustics in the church, it is a fantastic location for
concerts. The beautiful old barn in Ter Doest is also well worth a visit.'
For more information about 'the white village' see pages 76-77, 87 and 150.

The art of bobbins and pins

Kumiko Nakazaki hopes
to gain immortality through lace

It is now over a quarter-century since Kumiko Nakazaki from Japan
set foot in Bruges for the very first time. In the meantime, she has
blossomed into a true lace expert who understands like no one else
how important lace is for Bruges. It is no coincidence that the 2018 international lace congress will be held in Bruges.

At university, Kumiko Nakazaki specialised in French literature, more specifi-
cally the 19th century symbolic poets.
But she felt nothing for an academic ca-
reer. That is why she decided to go on
vacation for a year; to try and figure out
what direction she wanted to take with
her life. It was in the middle of this 'ca-
reer crisis' that she by chance attended
a Belgian exhibition about … lace.
'I learned that lace can grow very old,
can survive a very long time, and decided that I wanted to do something that
would live on for many years after my
death.' Straight away, Kumiko booked a
tour through Belgium, stopped for a day
in Bruges and ended up at the Lace
Centre, where she immediately made
clear that she would love to learn more
about lace-making. 'I returned to Japan
with the idea of living in Bruges and immediately applied for a student visa.'
At first, Kumiko found the change of
continents very difficult. 'During the
first years, you focus on the differences,

but after a while you start to notice simi-
larities.' As a result, she extended her
visa nine times! After almost a decade,
she had mastered the intricacies of
lace-making and designing. She had
even published a number of books about
lace. In other words, she had accom-
plished more than enough to leave Bru-

*'As long as skilled and passionate people want
to make lace and are prepared to continually learn,
Bruges will remain the world's undisputed lace capital.'*

ges, but she couldn't bring herself to do it. 'Bruges has become my second home, a part of my life. I now have many friends here. And so for years I have been shuttling back and forth between my Japanese home and Bruges. Sometimes I work in Japan, sometimes in Bruges. Both places give me everything I need: I can start working straight away in either of them, without losing any time. In fact, I do just the same things in Bruges as I do in Japan: drawing, drawing and more drawing. There is not much time left over to do anything else.'

Straddling the past and the future

'Whenever I shuttle between Belgium and Japan, I always ask myself over and over why I ever left in the first

LACE THROUGH THE CENTURIES

The history of lace in Belgium has its origins in the 16th century. It is generally assumed that bobbin lace was invented in Flanders, while needle lace probably originated in Venice. Whatever the truth of the matter, lace production became artistically, economically and socially important in Bruges in the years around 1550. The trade was protected and lace education was regulated. The religious orders (in particular, the nuns of Our Lady of Assumption and Our Lady of the Immaculate Conception) played a key role training poor girls to master the lace trade in special lace schools, where they also received a decent general education. In 1847, there were no fewer than 87 lace schools active in Bruges.

From 1850 onwards, lace-making evolved into a cottage industry. During the second half of the 19th century there were about 10,000 domestic lace-makers at work. This was exploitation on a massive scale; the lace merchants paid the women less than half of the average wage at the time. However, after the First World War the demand for hand-made lace fell dramatically and today lace-making is virtually non-existent as an economic activity. Fortunately, the people of Bruges managed to keep the old skills alive and have passed on this knowledge from generation to generation. Did you know that a simple method to learn lace-making was developed in the Bruges Lace College (founded in 1911) and that this method is now used all over the world? The lace techniques are taught by means of different colours: simple and the same in any language! Nowadays, various training courses are still organised in the Bruges Lace Centre, revealing the tricks of the lace trade to an increasing number of enthusiasts from every corner of the world.

You must not miss a visit to the permanent lace exhibition at the museum in the Lace Centre at Balstraat 16 (more info on page 85).

place. I love Bruges, because the city radiates enormous grandeur but is also easy to come to terms with. You can cross it by foot in less than an hour. Bruges is a city on a human scale – which is pure luxury for me. I also love New York and Tokyo, but only as a tourist. In those huge cities, everything is so much bigger and faster; they are also too modern for me. Bruges cherishes its past and its age-old lace tradition is an inextricably part of the city. Here, lace is not merely something you find in a museum or buy in a specialised shop; in Bruges, lace is part of daily life. Virtually every inhabitant of Bruges has lace somewhere in his house. I am convinced that there are still many lace treasures hidden in Bruges attics.'

In order to survive, the lace industry in Bruges must be more than just a fine

tradition. 'You have to strike the right balance. We need to respect the authentic traditions and the old techniques, but this is not enough; we must also dare to innovate and to give a more important place to creativity. With an open mind, without imposing any restrictions on ourselves, we must move forward towards the lace of tomorrow. The contemporary lace industry is standing with one foot in the past and one foot in the future.'

This is not always an easy position to be in – but Kumiko has managed it for decades. The Japanese lace expert successfully unites the two worlds: 'During my early years in Belgium, lace-making was a huge secret. It was an art that belonged to the city and was not to be shared. I was the first 'foreigner', for whom the lace door was opened. Since then, many dozens of lace enthusiasts from all over the world have followed lace courses in Bruges. And as long as skilled and passionate people want to make lace and are prepared to continually learn, Bruges will remain the world's undisputed lace capital.'

Kumiko Nakazaki
Best addresses

FAVOURITE SPOT

» **Prinselijk Begijnhof Ten Wijngaarde (Beguinage)**, tel. +32 (0)50 33 00 11

'Obviously I am not the only one who loves the **Beguinage**, with its white-painted houses and sober garden. It is a serene oasis in the middle of the city, a place in which you can find peace and contentment.' *(Also see pages 75-76)*

RESTAURANTS

» **'t Oud Handbogenhof**, Baliestraat 6, tel. +32 (0)50 33 71 18, www.hoteldepauw.be

'People have been eating at this site since the 15th century. And nothing much has changed. It is still the same atmospheric restaurant, where you can enjoy typical local cooking and seasonal dishes.'

» **Poules Moules**, Simon Stevinplein 9, tel. +32 (0)50 34 61 19, www.poulesmoules.be

'I only recently discovered this place: it is the address in Bruges for mussels, which is the specialty of the house. And if the weather permits, you can sit on the delightful terrace with its view of the Simon Stevinplein.'

» **De Pepermolen**, Langestraat 16, tel. +32 (0)50 49 02 25, www.depepermolen.com

'In this restaurant in the always bubbling Langestraat you can enjoy one of their seasonal dishes or try their monthly discovery menu. King crab, carpaccio of beef, fresh soused herrings... Need I say more?'

» **Tête Pressée**, Koningin Astridlaan 100, tel. +32 (0)470 21 26 27, www.tetepressee.be

'You can find this foodie paradise just outside the city centre, but Tête Pressée is well worth the small detour. You will have a fantastic meal, you can watch the chef in action, and afterwards buy your own supply of delicious things from the adjacent food store. A varied address that it is a delight to visit.'

» **De Middenstand**, 't Zand 20, tel. +32 (0)50 34 17 50, www.demiddenstand.com

'It's great to sit on the terrace overlooking the square 't Zand and just watch the world go by. This address is famous for its fresh home-made dishes. The owner of the restaurant is also the chef – which is always a good sign!'

CAFÉS AND TEAROOMS

» **Café Vlissinghe**, Blekersstraat 2, tel. +32 (0)50 34 37 37. www.cafevlissinghe.be

'This is one of the oldest pubs of the city. The beer has been flowing here since 1515 and the original medieval bar really takes you back in time. During the winter, it's great to gather around the warmth of the stove; during the summer, you can enjoy yourself on the outdoor terrace near the petanque court.'

» **Li O Lait**, Dweersstraat 30, tel. +32 (0)50 70 85 70, www.liolait.be

'A good breakfast, a filter coffee made grandma's way, a *mocha latte*, an ice coffee, a glass of cava, a bagel or a piece of cake... At any time of the day, you can enjoy yourself at Li O Lait.'

» **Tearoom Carpe Diem**, Wijngaardstraat 8, tel. +32 (0)50 33 54 47. www.tearoom-carpediem.be

'Located in a fabulous 17th century building near the Beguinage, you can enjoy the delights of the Detavernier Bakery and its attractive adjoining tearoom, where you can choose from their great selection of home-made cakes and other delicacies. It's a place where I enjoy coming to relax.'

» De IJsbeer, Noordzandstraat 73, tel. +32 (0)50 33 35 34, www.deijsbeer.be
'I only eat ice cream when I am in De IJsbeer, which has been making traditional Italian ice cream here since 1922. You can taste the freshness of the ingredients. Normally, I just stick to a cone with a couple of scoops of ice cream, but occasionally I treat myself to one of their delicious ice cream cups.'

» De Torre, Langestraat 8, tel. +32 (0)50 34 29 46, www.de-torre.com
'I like to drink a tea or coffee on the sunny terrace of De Torre, with its view of the Predikherenrei. And, having a sweet-tooth, I can almost never resist one of their delicious pancakes, waffles or a piece of apple pie.'

SHOPPING LIST

» Scharlaeken Handwerk,
Philipstockstraat 5, tel. +32 (0)50 33 34 55, www.scharlaeken.be

'If you like lace-making or embroidering, you will find your way blindfolded to this handiwork Valhalla. Scharlaeken Handwerk is specialised in lace-making, embroidery and knitting kits. There is also a fine selection of books, special linen, accessories and exclusive lace material.'

» 't Apostelientje, Balstraat 11, tel. +32 (0)50 33 78 60,
www.apostelientje.be
'For almost three decades, 't Apostelientje has been the place-to-be in Bruges for hand-made lace of the finest quality, offering an excellent choice of both contemporary and antique pieces. The service is both knowledgeable and helpful. True professionals at work!'

» The Lace Centre Shop, Balstraat 16, tel. +32 (0)50 33 00 72,
www.kantcentrum.eu
'Lace-lovers must visit the renovated (in 2014) Lace Centre, which is located in the old lace school once run by the Sisters of the Immaculate Conception. You can register to take part in a lace-making course and in the shop you can purchase beautiful pieces of lace and everything you need to make lace yourself.'
[See page 85]

>> **Ark van Zarren**, Zuidzandstraat 19, tel. +32 (0)50 33 77 28,
  www.arkvanzarren.be
'This is a great place to browse, right in the centre of town, where you can find different types of linen, fragrant soaps and special wallpapers. Romantic and rustic.'

>> **Rococo**, Wollestraat 9, tel. +32 (0)50 34 04 72, www.rococobrugge.be
'As long ago as 1833 Rococo was acquiring fame and fortune thanks to its unique lace creations. Nowadays, it specializes in the sale of traditional handcrafted lace work, both past and present. This is the address in Bruges for anyone who wants to buy antique lace. The shop also gives regular lace demonstrations and their expert staff will answer all your lace questions with great professionalism.'

SECRET TIP

>> **Saint Saviour's Cathedral**, Steenstraat, tel. +32 (0)50 33 61 88,
  www.sintsalvator.be
''Now that the Saint Saviour's Cathedral has finally been freed from its renovation scaffolding, it shines like never before. On the beautifully laid-out cathedral square, you can share the enjoyment of the children playing on the stone steps and the grassy lawns.' *For more information about the cathedral see page 91.*

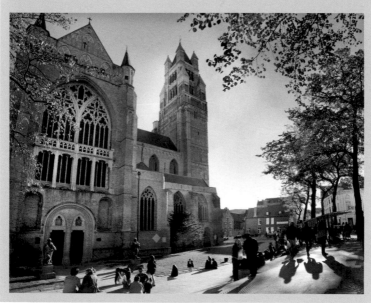

Photogenic Bruges

Andy McSweeney shows us the most beautiful spots in the city

His first visit to Bruges, now more than 18 years ago, made such an impression on Andy McSweeney, a Canadian with Irish roots, that he immediately fell in love with the beauty of the place - and decided to stay and marry a local girl. Nowadays, he guides photography enthusiasts who are still willing to learn around the city and shows them all the most photogenic spots.

ID-KIT

Name: Andy McSweeney
Nationality: Canadian
Date of birth: 8 December

Has lived in Bruges since 1999. Andy runs
Photo Tour Bruges. In this way, he combines
his love for Bruges with his love for photography.

It quickly became clear that Andy McSweeney, born in Montreal, was not destined to spend his whole life in Canada. At an early age, he drifted off to India, Australia and Europe, where, now more than a decade ago, he met his future wife in an Irish pub in Bruges. In almost every part of the world he has worked in catering, performed as a DJ ('I was the only one with good records') and... photographed the special places he encountered. During these wanderings he gradually trained himself to become a photographer, specializing in travel photography. 'Life as it is', perceived through a pair of keen eyes.

Andy soon left behind his catering and DJ life to concentrate fully on photography. And there is no better place to photograph time after time than Bruges. Nowadays, the Canadian organises photo tours through the city, in which he assists his clients with technical and artistic advice, while showing them all the most beautiful spots of Bruges. 'My strolls through the city are real workshops. Some of the participants are amateurs, trying to learn the basic tricks of the trade, whereas others are experienced photographers, who want to dis-

cover the most photogenic places the city has to offer. And there are plenty of those to keep them happy!' What's more, Andy McSweeney is convinced that Bruges is one of the best cities in the world to explore by camera. 'Bruges is a safe city. You don't have to be afraid that someone is going to steal your expensive camera. And the city has such beauty to offer, both past and present, at every moment of the day and in every season. While you are taking pictures,

day on the other side of the ocean he regards as an advantage. 'Anyone who is born and raised here is used to all the splendour from an early age, so that they find it harder to take a fresh look at the city. I have seen many other parts of the world, as a result of which I can probably see more easily than they can what makes this city so special. I am convinced that I can see things that they can't.'

The photographer – not the camera – determines the result

you look at the city with very different eyes and learn to focus on details that you might otherwise miss.'
The fact that Andy first saw the light of

When Andy is not busy taking groups around, you will regularly see him wan-

BRUGES ON THE BIG SCREEN

The fairytale-like and mysterious setting of Bruges has charmed numerous directors throughout the years. *The Nun's Story*, a movie from 1959 starring Audrey Hepburn, the prestigious British costume drama *The White Queen* (2013), the German romantic movie *Ein Herz aus Schokolade* (2010) and the Bollywood blockbuster *Peekay* (2014) were all shot in Bruges, as was the criminal comedy *In Bruges* (2008), which won several awards for its original script. Did you know that *Peekay* was the first Bollywood movie partially filmed in Belgium? Time and again the World Heritage city has been chosen as the setting for film productions or tourist shoots. The most popular filming locations are the courtyard of the Belfry, the Market Square with its Provincial Court, the Wijngaardplein, the Jerusalem Chapel and the Gothic Chamber of the Town Hall. In addition to the 'classics' (Rozenhoedkaai, Beguinage, Burg, Market Square, Minnewater and the canals), the tourist reports like to portray the lace-makers and chocolatiers of Bruges, as well as the windmills, the Church of Our Lady and the Holy Blood Basilica. Panoramic shots are taken from the roof of the Concert Hall or the Halve Maan Brewery. Tip: using the movie maps (available free of charge from the ℹ️ tourist information offices), you can visit the film locations shot in *Peekay*, *The White Queen* and *In Bruges*.

ANDY'S 5 MOST ROMANTIC PHOTOGRAPHIC HOTSPOTS

1. **Groenerei** (City map: F8) – A typical view of old bridges and historic buildings, framed by just a hint of nature.
2. **Koningin Astridpark** (City map: G9) – This classic park is a hidden gem, with its small pond with fountain and the colourful kiosk.
3. **Jan van Eyckplein** (City map: F6) –This was once the commercial heart of the city. Nowadays, it is a very pleasant spot to pass a few hours.
4. **Langerei** (City map: G3, F4 and F5) – Discover the essence of Bruges at the Langerei, one of the most photogenic canals in the city.
5. **Bonifaciusbrug** (City map: E9) – The charming and picturesque Bonifacius Bridge, with the Hof Arents alongside, never fails to charm visitors with its sense of history and romance.

Groenerei

dering through the city on his own, either on foot or on his recumbent bicycle.
'A part of my job is to search for new and interesting views. Bruges has a lot of imposing monuments and landmarks, but the trick is to find the best way to photograph them. I always try to maintain a fresh view and pass this on to my 'students'. You have to leave the beaten paths, because it is here, away from the hustle and bustle, that you will find the real magic. On the Jan van Eyckplein, for example, you can be inspired by the Flemish primitives. In the tranquil Sint-Anna district we focus on classic lines. The important thing is that you don't plan too far ahead, but just let the moment happen.' And he has some other tips for future photographers: 'You don't need to own an expensive camera to take beautiful pictures. It is not the car that matters, it's the driver. And be critical: don't show your friends twenty different pictures, but just a single fantastic shot. Then they'll probably want to come to Bruges next year as well!'
(For more information about the Photo Tour Brugge see page 69)

'Bruges has such beauty to offer, both past and present, at every moment of the day and in every season.'

Andy McSweeney
Best addresses

FAVOURITE SPOT

» **The Ramparts**

'I love **the Ramparts** surrounding the city and especially the stately windmills that remind us of past times. The turning sails exude a kind of peace and once you reach the top of the hill you are rewarded with a fantastic view over the city, all for free!'

RESTAURANTS

» **Blackbird**, Jan van Eyckplein 7, tel. +32 (0)50 34 74 44, www.blackbird-bruges.com

'Local people just love the Blackbird. It is always pleasantly busy, so it is a good idea to book in advance. I like to drop in for a delicious breakfast, but brunch or lunch at the Blackbird are also great. And no matter how often I come here, I always enjoy the elegant and refined interior.'

» **Parkrestaurant**, Minderbroedersstraat 1, tel. +32 (0)497 80 18 72, www.parkrestaurant.be

'The magnificent building housing the Park Restaurant is right on the edge of the Koningin Astridpark, one of the most romantic spots of Bruges. This restaurant offers Belgian cuisine with French influences.'

» Bierbrasserie Cambrinus, Philipstockstraat 19, tel. +32 (0)50 33 23 28, www.cambrinus.eu

'This beer brasserie honours its traditional Belgian roots. Here you can choose from an extensive range of 400 different Belgian beers, served with local dishes based on Belgian beers.'

» Bistro Pro Deo, Langestraat 161, tel. +32 (0)50 33 73 55, www.bistroprodeo.be

'A small workers house dating from 1562 now accommodates a cosy restaurant, frequented by both tourists and local people. In this bistro, you can enjoy traditional Belgian cuisine and fresh daily produce, made the way your grandmother used to make it.'

» In 't Nieuw Museum, Hooistraat 42, tel. +32 (0)50 33 12 80, www.nieuw-museum.com

'A classic address, both for fish fans and die-hard carnivores. Whatever you choose, everything is grilled exactly as it should be on a large charcoal fire. The pleasing rustic interior and a fine selection of top Belgian beers make the picture complete.'

CAFÉS

» L'Estaminet, Park 5, tel. +32 (0)50 33 09 16, www.estaminet-brugge.be

'A classic watering-hole for Bruges pub-hoppers. The interior is dressed up as an old-fashioned living room, where you can find excellent draft beer, good music and delicious bar food. In short, L'Estaminet has everything a good pub needs.'

» Vino Vino, Grauwwerkersstraat 15, tel. +32 (0)486 69 66 58
'A bluesy eatery where you immediately feel at home, thanks in no small measure to the delicious range of tapas, including fish and chips, squid, oven-baked camembert or patatas bravas. Good portions and excellent value for money. With plenty of good wine (and other things) to wash it all down.'

» Staminee De Garre, De Garre 1, tel. +32 (0)50 34 10 29, www.degarre.be
'This historic pub is hidden in the smallest street in Bruges and has a fine selection of delicious regional beers, as well as six draft beers, abbey beers, bottled beers and Trappist beers. Don't forget to try the tasty tapas.'

» Joey's Café, Zilversteeg 4, tel. +32 (0)50 34 12 64
'Local shoppers who have a sudden urge to hear a touch of the blues, jazz or rock, all hurry to this small 'brown' bar. It is located in the centre of the modern Zilverpand precinct, but is no less authentic for that. Concerts are regularly organised here.'

» 't Brugs Beertje, Kemelstraat 5, tel. +32 (0)50 33 96 16, www.brugsbeertje.be
'The Brugs Beertje is a genuine classic, professionally managed by Daisy. This is the perfect address for anyone who wants to immerse themselves in Belgian beer culture. The beers can be accompanied by local farmhouse pâté or a Belgian cheese platter.'

SHOPPING LIST

» The Lodge Bruges, Langestraat 50, tel. +32 (0)50 34 83 40

'In these hectic fashion times, The Lodge specialises in top quality men's clothing. Everything you buy here is practical, timeless – the garments last for years – but also solidly reliable and respectable: the clothes are made with honesty and respect for professional standards. The Lodge is primarily designed to cater to men, but women and children will also find something to tempt them here.'

» Dag en Zonne, Langestraat 3, tel. +32 (0)50 33 02 93
'There are sleek design stores and then there is Dag en Zonne, a boutique packed full with trinkets and antique knick-knacks that are a real treat for your eyes, even without you moving. If you don't find what you are looking for here, you won't find it anywhere.'

» LeeLoo, Sint-Jakobsstraat 19, tel. +32 (0)50 34 04 55, www.leeloo.be
'LeeLoo is not only a trendy city boutique, but a cool shop with a soul inspired by the alternative fashion scenes of London, Barcelona and Berlin. Clearly one step ahead of the rest.'

» Think Twice, Sint-Jakobsstraat 21, tel. +32 (0)495 36 39 08,
www.thinktwice-secondhand.be
'Vintage lovers and bargain hunters can browse for hours in this trendy second-hand shop that proves that nice outfits don't necessarily have to be expensive. Definitely a place to pop into on a regular basis.'

» Depot d'O, Riddersstraat 21, tel. +32 (0)495 23 65 95, www.depotdo.be
'In Depot d'O you can find great design classics, as well as African masks, zebra carpets, animal skulls and more unusual ornaments. It is a house of rarities, with a collection of objects that covers the entire world and an ever-changing display window. You have to be very quick, though.'

SECRET TIP

» Bruges during the winter
'For me, Bruges is at its most beautiful when it is covered in snow. In the winter, the city moves at a more relaxed pace, landscapes are transformed into frozen fairy tales and everywhere in the city you see smiling faces. In this way, Bruges becomes even more of a paradise for photographers!'

Lissewege

Discoveries outside of **Bruges**

The other Flemish historical cities

Antwerp (Antwerpen) 82 km

It is hard to describe Antwerp in a single word. This historic city has so much to offer: a beautiful cathedral and numerous imposing churches, a magnificent Central Station, the ground-breaking Museum on the River (MAS), the tranquil Rubens House, a delightful sculpture garden (Middelheim), a zoo with a history and so much more. Antwerp is also Belgium's fashion capital, home to many internationally renowned designers. That is why in the Scheldt city you will find dozens of exclusive boutiques, rubbing shoulders with fun bric-a-brac shops where you can browse for hours: it's every fashionista's dream! Not surprisingly, the local 'Antwerpenaars' – who are fairly loud by nature – are extremely proud of their city.

INFO > www.visitantwerpen.be; there is a direct train connection between Bruges and Antwerp (journey time: ca. 1.30 hours; www.belgianrail.be).

Brussels (Brussel) 88 km

The whole world comes together in Brussels, with a different continent around every corner. It is a city bursting with life, from the exotic Matonge quarter to the stately elegance of the European institutions. The capital of Belgium has a vibrancy like no other and the formality of its 'hard' metropolitan structure is softened by the authentic, working-class ambiance of its more popular districts. In the shadow of the majestic Market Square, *Manneken-Pis* is permanently peeing. And this diverse city even knows how to reconcile the chic sophistication of the Zavel with the folksy informality of the Vossenplein. Royalty watchers rush eagerly to the Paleizenplein, art lovers can do their thing at one of the more than

hundred museums and galleries, such as the Magritte Museum, the BOZAR (Museum of Fine Arts) or the Horta Museum, foodies hurry to the numerous food temples, and vintage-lovers climb to the top of the Atomium. And in the city where both Tintin and the Smurfs were born, comic lovers will have their every wish fulfilled, with more than 50 comic-strip walls and a renowned Comics Museum. **INFO >** visit.brussels; there is a direct train connection between Bruges and Bruxelles-Central (Brussels-Central, journey time: ca. 1.00 - 1.15 hours; www.belgianrail.be).

Damme   6 km

To the north-east of Bruges lies the charming town of Damme. Until the silting up of the tidal inlet Zwin, Damme was the transhipment port of Bruges. To reach the literary home of Tijl Uilenspiegel (Owlglass), you drive straight along the banks of the Damse Vaart (Damme Canal), which is without doubt one of the most beautiful pieces of nature in all Belgium. The canal is lined with magnificent poplars, some of which are over 100 years old. Their wind-

twisted trunks add to the charm of the setting. You can also experience their beauty from the water. The nostalgic paddle steamer *Lamme Goedzak* travels leisurely and in style to and fro between the small medieval town and Bruges' Noorweegse Kaai (Norwegian Quay). And every second Sunday of the month, Damme is transformed into a book centre, as booksellers from near and far come together to display their wares! **INFO >** www.toerismedamme.be; scheduled bus no. 43 (not on Saturday, Sunday and public holidays, see www.delijn.be for the time schedule), bus stop: Damme Plaats; or by the paddle steamer Lamme Goedzak, www.bootdamme-brugge.be *(For more information see page 67)*. You can also easily cycle to Damme *(for bicycle rental points see pages 12-13)* or hire a scooter to ride there *(see pages 20-21 for scooter rental points)*.

Ghent (Gent)   39 km

No other people are as stubborn and as self-willed as the people of Ghent – or the Gentenaars, as they are known. It is built into their genes. In the Middle Ages, the 'Gentenaars' revolted against Emperor

Charles V and later they formed the first trade union, but they also built many great monuments and churches. You can admire the magnificent *Lamb of God* altarpiece by the van Eyck brothers in Saint Bavo's Cathedral. Before you settle down on one of the many terraces on the Graslei or the Korenlei, make sure you first have a look at the majestic belfry, the much-discussed city hall and the old town hall. And don't forget to check out the Gravensteen and the lively district of winding medieval streets known as Patershol, which lies at the foot of the great castle. The House of Alijn, the Ghent Design Museum, the S.M.A.K. (Museum of Contemporary Art) and the STAM (Ghent City Museum) are all outstanding and groundbreaking museums. The same words could also be used to describe Ghent's large student population and the colourful vibe they create in the city's nightlife and cultural scene. With its young and creative star-rated chefs and its reputation as the veggie capital of Europe, Ghent is also a city for food-lovers of every kind. The highlight of the year is the Gentse Feesten, Europe's largest city festival, which is organised annually in mid-July and sets the city alight!

INFO > www.visitgent.be; there is a direct train connection between Bruges and Ghent (Sint-Pieters) (journey time: ca. 30 min.; www.belgianrail.be).

you come across students everywhere, moving from one campus to another. Leuven can proudly boast the largest and oldest university in Belgium, founded as long ago as 1425. Notwithstanding its long history, Leuven is always open to innovation, as can be seen in several remarkable architectural projects, such as the station, the Stuk Art Centre, Het Depot, De Hoorn (The Horn) in the trendy Vaartkom district and the M-Museum. And then there is Leuven, city of beer. With two breweries – the giant Stella Artois plant and the smaller, more local Domus brewery – located in the city centre and with several other traditional brewers nearby, there is no excuse not to relax for a few moments with a foaming pint. And what better place than on the Oude Markt (Old Market), possibly the world's longest bar...

INFO > www.visitleuven.be; there is a direct train connection between Bruges and Leuven (journey time: ca. 1.30 hours; www.belgianrail.be).

Louvain (Leuven)   110 km

Louvain is without a doubt the number one student city in Belgium. Dozens of historic university buildings are spread all over the old city centre. As a result,

Malines (Mechelen)   90 km

Although the smallest of the Flemish art cities, Mechelen is well worth a visit. Situated halfway between Antwerp and Brussels, Mechelen is more compact

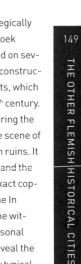

than these major players, but still has its fair share of wonderful historic buildings. The most well-known landmark is the proud St. Rombout's Cathedral. Its 97-metre high tower contains two sets of bells, which are regularly played by pupils of the Mechelen carillon school – the oldest and largest in the world. In addition, the River Dijle meanders through the city, enclosed by the Zoutwerf (Salt Quay) with its 16th century wooden frontages and the Haverwerf (Oat Quay) with its pastel-coloured decorative facades. The imposing Lamot brewery complex nowadays serves as a congress and heritage centre and is beautifully renovated in a daring and contemporary architectural style. Another must-see is the Palace of Margaret of Austria, from where the Netherlands were once governed.

INFO > www.visitmechelen.be; there is a train connection between Bruges and Mechelen, with a single change of trains in Gent-Sint-Pieters or Bruxelles-Midi (Brussels-South) (journey time: ca. 1.30 - 1.45 hours; www.belgianrail.be).

Ypres (Ieper)   46 km

Thanks to its flourishing cloth industry, Ypres, along with Bruges and Ghent, was one of the most powerful cities in Flanders in the 13th century. Its strategically important position in the Westhoek meant that the city was besieged on several occasions, resulting in the construction of strong defensive ramparts, which were further extended in the 17th century. Ypres also paid a heavy price during the First World War, when it was the scene of fierce fighting that left the city in ruins. It was rebuilt after the Armistice, and the most important buildings are exact copies of the medieval originals. The In Flanders Fields Museum lets the witnesses of war tell their own personal stories. These little histories reveal the huge emotions that are so sadly typical of all conflict. This allows visitors to experience the horror of the trenches and the bombardment of the city. Various (day) trips are organized from Bruges to Ypres and other sites of interest in the Westhoek *(see pages 157-159).*

INFO > www.visitieper.be; there is a train connection between Bruges and Ypres, with a single change of trains in Kortrijk (journey time: ca. 1.30 hours; www.belgianrail.be); from Ypres station, it is approximately a 10-minute walk to the main Market Square.

The area around Bruges

BRUGES' WOOD- AND WETLAND

The Bruges' wood- and wetland is a green region surrounding the city. It is the ideal place to press the 'pause' button for a moment, allowing the stresses of daily life to gently fade away. Here, the clock ticks just a little more slowly and the good life is all that counts. Perhaps for this reason, the 'Ommeland' is home to several star-rated chefs, as well as numerous passionate regional producers. The pleasing canals, the open polders (that encourage cycling towards the coast) and the many historic buildings set amidst the greenery all add up to make a captivating region of great beauty and simplicity. The world heritage city of Bruges is the beating heart of the region, but the surrounding villages and small towns, steeped in old-world charm, are its soul. You can wander around in castles or soak up history in Damme and Lissewege. In fact, there is so much to do that you will be spoilt for choice!
INFO > www.brugseommeland.be

In the Bruges' wood- and wetland, you can visit: the Uilenspiegel Museum (Damme, 6 km, www.toerismedamme. be), the home of Tijl Uilenspiegel and his Nele; the Lamme Goedzak (Damme,

6 km, www.bootdamme-brugge.be *(see also page 67)*, a nostalgic paddle steamer that sails between Bruges and Damme; Loppem Castle (Loppem, 6 km, www.kasteelvanloppem.be), where King Albert I resided during the liberation of Belgium at the end of the First World War; the Permeke Museum (Jabbeke, 10 km, www.muzee.be), where you can stroll around the home, garden and workshops of the renowned painter Constant Permeke; the Roman Archaeological Museum (Romeins Archeologisch Museum - RAM) (Oudenburg, 16 km, www.ram-oudenburg.be), where you can marvel at the archaeological finds from Oudenburg's glorious past; Wijnendale castle (Torhout, 18 km, www.toerismetorhout.be), home to more than 1,000 years of history and a place of sad

Wijnendale

Damse Vaart

TIP

The ideal way to discover the sourroundings of Bruges is by bike. Make your own route using the new cycle network maps or follow the signposted Groene Gordel (Green Belt) cycle route.
(See pages 12-13 for bicycle rental points)

memories for King Leopold III; and the Torhout Pottery Museum (Torhout, 18 km, www.toerismetorhout.be), which focuses on the rich tradition of the worldfamous Torhout earthenware.

COAST

The Coast never loses its appeal; it always has something for everyone. From De Panne to Knokke-Heist, each seaside resort has its own unique atmosphere. Old-world or contemporary, picturesque or chic, intimate or urbane, the seaside towns are all purveyors of the good life. Nature galore, an abundance of culture, wonderful sandy beaches, inviting shopping streets, traffic-free promenades that are ideal for a bracing seaside stroll: this is the Coast in a nutshell! And the regular tram service (www.dekusttram.be) allows you to travel from one resort to another in no time at all. Taste that salty sea air, enjoy the mild climate and treat yourself to a delicious meal with the very best the North Sea has to offer. You know it makes sense!
INFO > www.dekust.be

You must certainly not miss out on a visit to Seafront (Zeebrugge, 14 km, www.seafront.be, *see pages 88-89*), a maritime theme park where you will discover all secrets of the sea; the Port Cruise (Zeebrugge, 14 km, www.franlis.be; *see pages 67-68*), where you will explore one of Europe's busiest ports on the passenger boat *Zephira*, taking in one of the world's largest locks along the way; the Mu.ZEE Oostende Museum of Fine Art (Ostend,

Zeebrugge

22 km, www.muzee.be), with its unique collection of modern and contemporary Belgian art, and the Ensor House (Ostend, 22 km, www. muzee.be), where you can enter into the fascinating world of Ostend's most famous painter.

Zeebrugge, Seafront

WESTHOEK

Endless panoramas, gently rolling hills, open polders and breath-taking silence. Once a battlefield of the Great War, now a peaceful and truly authentic holiday destination. In the Westhoek you will discover tranquil villages, steeped in history. An ideal place for great walks and hours of cycling fun, with delightful inns and charming restaurants at the most idyllic spots, far away from the hustle and bustle of daily life. Just sit back and enjoy a stiff glass of *picon*, the tasty aperitif so typical of this border region, sandwiched between the French frontier and the North Sea coast. And wherever you go, you are guaranteed to get a warm Westhoek welcome. From

Bruges, various (day) trips are organised to the Westhoek *(see pages 157-159)*. **INFO >** www.toerismewesthoek.be, www.flandersfields.be

Among the things you definitely have to see are the In Flanders Fields Museum (Ypres, 46 km, www.inflandersfields.be), which tells the historic story of the First World War in the West Flanders front region in a highly impressive way; Tyne Cot Cemetery (Passendale, 54 km, www.passchendaele.be, www.cwg.org), where the terrible human cost of the First World War is given concrete expression in the largest Commonwealth military cemetery on the continent; and the Last Post Ceremony (Ypres, 46 km, www.lastpost.be), which has paid daily tribute to the fallen soldiers every evening since 1928 at 8 o'clock sharp under the Menin Gate Memorial.

Passendale, Tyne Cot Cemetery

Courtrai

From Lisbourg in France to the centre of Ghent, the Lys winds its way through a varied landscape. The flax industry created prosperity and transformed the Lys Valley into a dynamic centre of economic activity, focused on small and pleasant cities like Roulers (Roeselare), Waregem, Deinze and Courtrai (Kortrijk). The various museums in the eastern part of the Lys region are also well worth a visit. The gently rolling landscape between the Lys and the Scheldt is ideal for exploring on foot, by bike or even by boat (there are several boat rental companies active locally). And whatever your mode of transport, why not take a relaxing break at the riverside and enjoy one of the typical red-brown beers that are only brewed in this part of the world.

INFO > www.toerisme-leiestreek.be

Make sure you visit Texture (Courtrai, 44 km, www.texturekortrijk.be), a museum where you will learn everything about the Lys and its flax industry; Kortrijk 1302 (Courtrai, 44 km, www.kortrijk1302.be), where you will be catapulted back in time to the days of Flanders' most famous battle, which also has a Bruges connection, and the Deinze and Leie Regional Museum (Deinze, 47 km, www.museumdeinze.be), whose collection includes (among other things) works by Emile Claus, Constant Permeke and Raoul De Keyser, as well as offering a complete overview of the famous Leie school of artists from 1875 to the present day.

MEETJESLAND: FLANDERS CREEK COUNTRY

Assenede

The Meetjesland is a region of ancient creeks and ponds, close to the Dutch border. During the First World War, the famous 'Dodendraad' (Wire of Death) ran across this region, but nowadays it is a haven of peace and quiet. Nowhere more so than in Sint-Laureins, where you can enjoy a delicious meal while taking in the spectacular views. Pull on your walking shoes and explore the

'Meetjeslandse kreken' (creeks) and/or the 'Meetjeslandse bossen' (woods) routes. More energetic visitors can explore the region around Eeklo by bike, making use of the extensive cycling networks and pausing to admire the forests, heather and peatlands in the Drongengoed landscape park. Really enthusiastic cyclists can press on to Het Leen nature reserve, or even follow the River Lieve as far as Ghent.

INFO > www.toerismemeetjesland.be

Well worth a visit: Canada-Poland War Museum (Adegem, 19 km, www. canadamuseum.be), a double museum that reflects on daily life in Belgium during the Second World War and also tells the story of the region's Polish and Canadian liberators, and the Maldegem Steam Train Centre (Maldegem, 18 km, www.stoomcentrum.be), where you can take a ride on an authentic steam or diesel train.

FLEMISH ARDENNES

The woodlands of the Flemish Ardennes conceal a surprisingly undulating landscape, ideal for exploring on foot or by bike. The tree-topped hills, the wonderful panoramas and the cobbled roads over which the cycling classics are raced annually offer an infinite variety of opportunities for tourists of all kinds. Admire the spectacular view from the summit of the Kluisberg, relax on the 'mountain' slopes in the Kluisbos recreational park or test the steepness of the notorious Koppenberg hill. Lovers of culture, heritage and gastronomy will be able to

indulge themselves to the full in this charming region between Audenarde (Oudenaarde), Zottegem, Geraardsbergen and Ronse.

INFO > www.toerismevlaamse ardennen.be

In this region you have just got to take in the Centrum Ronde van Vlaanderen (Tour of Flanders Centre), (Oudenaarde, 49 km, www.crvv.be), a unique visitor and experience centre that tells the heroic story of Flanders' most famous cycling race, and the Museum of Oudenaarde and the Flemish Ardennes (MOU) (Oudenaarde, 49 km, www.mou-oudenaarde. be), which is housed in the beautiful town hall and boasts, among other things, one of the largest collections of silver in Flanders.

Audenarde, Centrum Ronde van Vlaanderen

Guided excursions from Bruges

BY BIKE

The Green Bike Tour

A guided trip to the polders, the flat countryside around Bruges. The tour pulls up at medieval Damme and other important sights along the way for a little extra commentary. Tandem tours, with a search game and a number of fun dexterity tests, can also be arranged.

OPEN > Daily excursions, by appointment only. Reservation is required.
PRICE > € 18.00 (bike) or € 36.00 (tandem); children under 12: € 11.00; € 9.00 if you bring your own bike
MEETING POINT > Concertgebouw, on 't Zand
LANGUAGES > English, Dutch, French, German (but not for the tandem tours)
INFO AND RESERVATION > Tel. +32 (0)50 61 26 67, arlando@telenet.be

The Pink Bear Bike Tours

A mere five minutes away from bustling Bruges lies one of the prettiest rural areas in Europe. You ride to historic Damme, the handsome medieval market town, once Bruges' outpost. Furthermore, a guide will show you the most enchanting places of the Polders. It goes without saying that there is also a stop at a pleasant café for some Belgian Beers

Damme

and/or Belgian waffles. On your return you follow the beautiful poplar planted banks of a canal and discover some of Bruges' best-kept secrets.

OPEN > Daily excursions, by appointment only. Reservation is required.
PRICE > € 27.00; youngsters aged 9 to 26: € 25.00; children under 9: free; € 18.00 if you bring your own bike
MEETING POINT > Belfry, on the Markt
LANGUAGES > English, but on request also Dutch or French
INFO AND RESERVATION > Tel. +32 (0)50 61 66 86 or +32 (0)476 74 45 25, www.pinkbear.freeservers.com

NEW Steershop

For an active morning's cycling, why not try a tour with the trendy Steershop? A ride to the coast, a visit to Damme or a fun off-road tour through the wonderful woods around Bruges: it's all possible! The day starts with a light breakfast. And if you want to, you can keep your bike until later the same evening, so that you can continue your explorations in the afternoon at your own pace.

OPEN > Daily excursion, 9.00 a.m.–1.00 p.m. By appointment only for a minimum of 5 persons. Reservation is required.

PRICE > Including bike (for the whole day), guide (just in the morning), breakfast and welcome coffee: € 40.00; € 15.00 if you bring your own bike.

MEETING POINT > Steershop, Havenstraat 3

LANGUAGES > English, Dutch, French

INFO AND RESERVATION > Tel. +32 (0)474 40 84 01, www.steershop.be

QuasiMundo Biketours: The Hinterland of Bruges by bike

A tour through Bruges' wood- and wetlands, passing through medieval towns such as Damme, peaceful Flemish agrarian villages and dead straight canals. A must-do for anyone who loves the peaceful greenery of the countryside.

Damme

OPEN > Excursions during the period 1/4 to 15/10: daily, 1.00 p.m.–5.00 p.m. Reservation is required.

PRICE > Including bike, guide, raincoat and refreshment in a local café: € 30.00; youngsters aged 9 to 26 and students: € 28.00. If you bring your own bike you pay € 18.00 as an adult or € 16.00 as a youngster (aged 9 to 26) or a student; children under 9: free

MEETING POINT > At the town hall on Burg Square, 10 minutes before departure

LANGUAGES > English, other languages on request

INFO AND RESERVATION > Tel. +32 (0)50 33 07 75 or +32 (0)478 28 15 21, www.quasimundo.eu

(See also 'Exploring Bruges', page 71)

BY MINIBUS

Triple Treat Quasimodo tour: The best of Belgium in one day

Take it easy on this minibus tour, which takes you to, amongst others, the illustrious Tilleghem Castle and unique Neo-Gothic Loppem Castle. Included are a pleasant stroll through medieval Damme and a visit to the Gothic abbey barn of Ter Doest at Lissewege. And what would this tour be without some delicious waffles and mouth-watering chocolate? The tour ends with a visit to the Fort Lapin Brewery, just outside of Bruges.

OPEN > Excursions during the period 1/3 to 31/10: on Monday, Wednesday and

Friday. Reservation is required.

PRICE > Including guide, lunch and tickets for Loppem Castle and the Fort Lapin Brewery: € 67.50; youngsters aged 7 to 25: € 57.50; there is an immediate € 10.00 reduction when you also book the Quasimodo WWI Flanders Fields Tour *(see pages 157-158)*.

MEETING POINT > You will be picked up wherever you are staying or at a pick-up spot in the centre of Bruges. Departure: 9.00 a.m. Return: 5.00 p.m.

LANGUAGE > English

Loppem Castle

INFO AND RESERVATION > Tel. 0800 975 25 or +32 (0)50 37 04 70, www.quasimodo.be

BY VESPA

Vespa Tours

Discover Bruges' Hinterland in style: book a guided tour with a snazzy Vespa scooter and traverse the green polders, authentic villages and breath-taking landscapes. A couple of surprises are provided en route. You can also opt for the *Cook & Drive a Vespa* arrangement, a daylong programme with a fun mix of cooking and sightseeing.

If you prefer to explore the surrounding area of Bruges unaccompanied, you can also hire a Vespa *(see page 21)*.

OPEN > Excursions during the period 1/3 to 31/10: daily, 10.00 a.m.-6.00 p.m.

Reservation is required.

PRICE PER VESPA > Including helmet(s), guide and insurance: half day tour: € 65.00 (1 person) or € 80.00 (2 persons); day tour: € 100.00 (1 person) or € 115.00 (2 persons)

MEETING POINT > Estaminet 't Molenhuis, Potterierei 109

LANGUAGES > English, Dutch, French

CONDITIONS > Minimum age of driver: 21 years, driving licence B, deposit of € 200.00 to be paid before departure

INFO AND RESERVATION > Tel. +32 (0)497 64 86 48, www.vespatours-brugge.be

TO THE BATTLEFIELDS

Quasimodo WWI Flanders Fields Tour

Experience with Quasimodo Tours a personal and memorable trip to Passendale, Hill 60, Messines Ridge, the

private museum at Hooge Crater in Zillebeke, several Commonwealth and German cemeteries, trenches and bunkers, the Menin Gate and numerous Australian, New Zealand, Canadian,

British and Irish monuments. In short, all the highlights! The stories told by the Quasimodo Tours allow you to visualize the reality of four terrible years of war in the Ypres Salient. It is also possible to stay on in Ypres after the tour has ended, so that you can attend the Last Post ceremony at 8.00 p.m. In this case, you will be brought back to Bruges by taxi after the ceremony.

OPEN > Excursions during the period 1/2 to 31/12: Tuesday to Sunday. Reservation is required.

PRICE > Including guide, lunch and ticket Hooge Crater Museum: € 67.50; youngsters aged 7 to 25: € 57.50; there is an immediate € 10.00 reduction when you also book the Triple Treat Quasimodo tour: The best of Belgium in one day *(see pages 156-157)*. People who opt to stay for the Last Post must pay the cost of the taxi ride separately.

MEETING POINT > You will be picked up wherever you are staying or at a pick-up spot in the centre of Bruges. Departure: 9.00 a.m. Return: ca. 6.00 p.m.

LANGUAGE > English

INFO AND RESERVATION > Tel. 0800 975 25 or +32 (0)50 37 04 70, www.quasi

modo.be. Tickets are also available from the ℹ tourist offices on 't Zand (Concertgebouw) and the Markt (Historium).

In Flanders Fields tour

This bus tour will take you to numerous sites of interest related to the war of 1914-1918. You will visit the *Grieving Parents* by Käthe Kollwitz in Vladslo, the trenches along the River IJzer, the John McCrae site at Essex Farm Cemetery near Boezinge and the mine craters at Hill 60. The trip also takes you to a number of remarkable war monuments: the Canadian *Brooding Soldier* (Sint-Juliaan), the French Guynemer monument (Poelkapelle) and the New Zealand Memorial in Passendale. The French military cemetery at Saint Charles de Potyze (just outside Ypres), the Belgian military cemetery at Houthulst and the world's largest Commonwealth military cemetery at Tyne Cot (near Passendale) are also included in the itinerary. The day is rounded off with a visit to the In Flanders Fields Museum in Ypres and the Last Post ceremony at the Menin Gate.

OPEN > Excursions during the period 7/4 to 27/10: Thursday and Sunday, and also on 5/11 and 11/11

PRICE > Including guide, lunch and ticket to the In Flanders Fields Museum: € 76.00; 65+ and students aged 13 to 26: € 69.00; children aged 6 to 12: € 38.00

Last Post

Vladslo

MEETING POINT > You are collected from the bus stop at the Bargeplein/'Kanaal-eiland': 10.15 a.m. Return: 9.30 p.m.

LANGUAGES > English, French

INFO AND RESERVATION > Tel. +32 (0)2 513 77 44, www.brussels-city-tours.be, www.ticketsbrugge.be. Tickets are also available from the **i** tourist offices on 't Zand (Concertgebouw) and the Markt (Historium).

Flanders Fields Battlefield Daytours

Discover the most popular tourist attractions of the Westhoek and the Great War. You will visit the German cemetery at Langemark, Tyne Cot Cemetery in Passendale, the Memorial Museum Passchendaele 1917 in Zonnebeke, where you can enjoy a dugout-tunnel experience, the Menin Gate, the City of Ypres with its magnificent Cloth Hall and the not-to-be-missed In Flanders Fields Museum. The tour continues to Hill 60, Hill 62 (craters and bunkers), Heuvelland and Kemmelberg, Messines Ridge, the mine craters of 7 June 1917, trenches and various other war monuments.

OPEN > Excursions from Tuesday to Sunday

ADDITIONAL CLOSING DATES > No excursions during the period 10/1 to 31/1

PRICE > Including guide, lunch, a local beer and tickets to the In Flanders Fields Museum and the Memorial Museum Passchendaele 1917: € 75.00; students aged 18 to 26: € 72.00; youngsters aged 12 to 17: € 70.00; children aged 8 to 11: € 60.00; children under 8: free

MEETING POINT > You are collected from your hotel. Departure: 8.30 a.m.-8.45 a.m. Return: 5.15 p.m.

LANGUAGES > English, Dutch, French, German

ON REQUEST > Short evening trip to the Last Post ceremony at the Menin Gate in Ypres. Departure: 6.15 p.m. Return: 9.15 p.m. Price: € 45.00. It is also possible to combine the day tour with an evening trip or to make special made-to-measure excursions (also abroad) to suit your specific requirements.

INFO AND RESERVATION > Tel. +32 (0)800 99 133, www.visitbruges.org

Index of street names